UNLOCKING THE

DEBORAH

IN YOU

Discovering the leader WITHIN…

The Traits of a Great Female Leader

SANDRA EKPENYONG

JOSEPH DREAM
PUBLISHING CO.

Unlocking the Deborah in You; Discovering the Leader Within

First Edition
Women Empowerment/Christian Leadership/Self-help/General

To purchase or contact the author:-

Sandra Ekpenyong
Email: publisher@josephdreampublishing.com

UNLOCKING THE

DEBORAH

IN YOU

Discovering the leader WITHIN...

The Traits of a Great Female Leader

SANDRA EKPENYONG

JOSEPH DREAM
PUBLISHING CO.

Other books by Sandra Ekpenyong

Biblical Dysfunctional Families That Made It!

Biblical Dysfunctional Families That Made It
(Mini-book series)

Woman... God Has Given You Your Voice BACK!

Unlocking the Deborah in You (18 Week Journal)

Igniting Your Vision and Beyond

The Father-Daughter Relationships of the Bible

Jealousy, the Spirit of Destruction

Oh Lord!!!! Who Have I Married (Men/Women)

The Samson Story that was NEVER told

The Different Christian Faith Process

And many more...

Table of Contents

Foreword

In every generation and in every era, God calls a woman, who, against all odds, rises above the order of her day to make a difference, blaze a trail, put her name in the annals of time, "dig a well" that generations after her would drink from Deborah was such a women. There is no time like ours where women have been given a voice to make an impact in the world. However, with such awesome privileges comes attached real challenges and great responsibility to continually equip the women of our generation to take their place in their various leadership roles and make a difference, whether it is in the home or in the marketplace. *"Unlocking the Deborah In You, Discovering the Leader Within"* is a compact manual, a tool, for leadership development and success for women everywhere. In fact, this book can serve as a training manual for the personal growth and leadership development of women of all walks of life.

The golden nuggets of leadership principles imbedded in every chapter of this book can become the *"yeast"* in the *"dough of our lives,"* and if we would work them into our lives until the "whole dough is affected," what we would be left with would be changed lives, purpose realized, destiny fulfilled, and our world transformed. What is evident is that Deborah was an extraordinary woman of her time, but so are you reading this book. If you would take the principles that Sandra Ekpenyong puts in this book and work them into your life, you too will leave your footprints on the seashores of life that will show generations of women to come that God can uses ordinary women to do extraordinary things. Read, study, confess, implement the principles in this book, and the great leader in you will begin to emerge. Discover you and just do it.

AleroTebu
Director of Ministry
Dayspring International

Introduction

Inside of every woman is a Deborah waiting to be unlocked to achieve great things. There is a leader begging to be discovered by her peers, nations, or even family. A hidden treasure that the whole world is depending on to answer her call; but it will take a willingness to rise and walk in your God-given authority. This means it is your responsibility to rise and release the Deborah inside of you to become a leader. Many women throughout the Bible had been overlooked by people but had been endorsed by God. Women everywhere have the potential of becoming great leaders no matter whether they are housewives, career women, single, married or even students.

Deborah, the first female general ever mentioned in the Bible, had a lot of strikes against her, but she refused to allow anything or anyone to handicap her. She knew how to use her strength and that of others, and she encouraged the gifts of them who were both near to and far from her. This trailblazer of a woman who had no female mentor to guide her, still allowed God to use her to fulfill His mission. Apart from being a prophetess, she was a career woman and a wife, sister and daughter. Throughout history, women have always contributed to the advancement of mankind, but God is also interested in raising up women leaders as well.

It will take a woman to discover the leader within her; Esther found the courage to confront her people's enemy, Haman, while the daughters of Zelophehad faced Moses and the whole congregation to gainfully secure their inheritance. While Ruth was willing to lie at Boaz's feet, Abigail averted the destruction of her home through the medium of diplomacy. Every woman has the potential to become a great leader if she can locate the Deborah within her. Where there is a crisis, there is an opportunity, and where there is need, God plants a woman to become that seed. Somewhere inside of you is a Deborah trying to come out, let God use her to fulfill her purpose... stand up and answer the call of Deborah!

Sandra Ekpenyong

The Making of a Leader

Deborah is unlike many of the other women leaders in the Bible because she is the first general and only female judge of her time. The odds were pretty much stacked up against her in many ways, but one thing for sure was that she was underestimated as a woman. Every great leader must overcome specific challenges and face certain obstacles to become respected by her peers, and Deborah was no different. Whether it was the issue of her gender, career, inexperience, or the simple shortcomings of those who surrounded her, she did not allow any of these things to stop her.

Unassuming leaders tend to fall victim to different types of biases; Ruth because she was a Moabitess and a young widow, Rahab a prostitute, and Esther the new young wife, and so did Deborah! When a leader is unappreciated for her gifts, it causes her to become stagnant and unable to reach the pinnacle of success that God has prepared for her. It is the very reason why in one ministry a congregation is inactive, and in another ministry they suddenly rise to stardom. Like many women, Deborah had a choice to make and she made the right one by stepping out by faith. The best of leaders have at one time been prejudged or misjudged in their careers, ministries, or by their families.

Half-truths, folktales, and certain biases have prevented many women from using their gifts for the kingdom, in the marketplaces or at home. Satan has successfully campaigned against women, telling them that they can only operate in the office of a Sunday school teacher, children's ministry, or church building committee! Until women wake up, we will continue to take baby steps instead of taking giants ones. The fact is the one is who is grossly underrated normally has the greatest of gifts! A gift is an asset of value, worth or something that has endless possibilities or opportunities attached to it. Deborah was unquestionably a great asset to God's people, not only as an emerging spiritual leader and judge, but also as a woman.

She rose above the challenges of her gender to lead her people into a win over Sisera. In an age when women did not hold any leadership position, she was able to hold her own with boldness and calculating acumen, proving to all that she was not afraid of anyone. If she had fears, she never showed it; if she had doubts about her decisions, she hid them. This great woman refused to allow her gender to be used against her, but rather employed it to encourage women to rise up and make a difference. What makes a leader great is their ability not just to get the work done, but to encourage those who are around them.

They must have persistence, solutions, strategies, and be able to operate well under pressure. A good leader should have a healthy amount of critics but should also have a few trusted allies as well. Deborah does great as a leader, and it will do us all well as women to take a page out of her extraordinary life as a leader and learn from her. God has a great plan for women leaders, and He alone knows where to tactically place us, whether it be in ministry, marketplace, or within the family.

Your focus should not be whether you are the least, as biblical history teaches us that it is the ordinary people who can make a world of difference. The victory of Israel was secured by a homemaker using simple household tools! What do you see concerning your future and will you discover your personal value? What will history have to say about you? You are responsible for you and the tools that God has given to you to be an asset to the Kingdom. This book is for women who are not afraid of becoming a leader. What about you?

The Eighteen Attributes of Deborah the Leader....

Chapter One

Deborah, the Leader

When the leaders lead in Israel
When the people willingly offer themselves
Bless the Lord... Judges 5:2

> ℰⓇ
>
> **GREAT LEADERS ARE PROACTIVE WHILE POOR LEADERS ARE REACTIVE.**
>
> ℰⓈ

Deborah knew that great leadership starts with good and godly leaders. Leaders who can hear from God as well as lead His people are just scratching the surface. They must learn not only to share their vision but take charge of it as well. The vision and the mission must be shared with the masses effectively. Failure to do so will only lead to confusion, conflict, and panic among the people. Once there is inconsistency, resistance is next to follow, and then division. Leaders lead and not the people, as Deborah's song duly notes.

Poor leadership shrugs off their responsibility for someone else to handle who has not been given the proper insight or guidance to what the Lord desires to achieve. Israel was in a chaotic mess because the leadership was morally bankrupt. This in turn gave people the liberty to shake off their restraints. When leaders blatantly refuse to take up their roles, the masses feel as though they can do anything and get away with it. A leader who lacks integrity will eventually fail in her ability to lead. The conduct of any leader is just as important as her vision and her direction.

Whenever a leader lacks character, it jeopardizes everything that her people have worked for. Queen Jezebel had a great opportunity to lead her husband's people but chose destruction instead of construction. She single-handedly led to the spiritual and moral decay of Israel. Good leadership guides yet allows liberty, equips but permits originality, provides but understands that there will be mistakes; corrects with love and walks in forgiveness. A true sign of proper leadership introduces growth and innovation coupled with restraints, laws, and accountability.

Bad character can hurt the best of leaders even when their vision is groundbreaking and fresh. A visionary with questionable character will never get or retain the best skilled people needed to get their vision fulfilled. Great leaders are proactive while poor leaders are reactive. While the initial stage of any new venture has hiccups along the way, informed leaders have fewer fires to put out versus uninformed ones. Decision-making is easier when there is a constant flow of information. Allowing room for the Holy Spirit to guide is especially important. When leaders react like everyone else, it shows that they are not in control of the situation.

Deborah proved herself a great leader by adequately using the data she had been given to wage an effective faith-based war against Sisera. A leader should prepare herself for information she might not like; it is still relevant in helping make the right decisions. Great leadership takes what she has and produces with it the result she desires to best help her people. A good leader must sacrifice herself for her people. Failure in doing so will cause people to begin to bail out on your vision; people must know that you are ready to give as much as they are in achieving your dreams.

Seasoned leaders know the power of unifying people to one common cause or goal. A great leader must sell her vision effectively, making her a great saleswoman. She must tell her people the price of the vision and inspire them to believe in it and make the sacrifice. When the leader and the people share the same cause, victory is inevitable. Deborah effectively pitched her war idea to a bunch of rebellious people and a failed general and won. Every leader does not necessarily get the type of people that she wants, so she must learn to build and mold those who are willing into capable followers.

Great leaders can inspire the faithless and the tired. This is probably the most difficult thing that Deborah had to do as a leader. She had to deal with the other tribes abandoning them, as well as faithless people, including a wishy-washy general. She had the responsibility of trying to win the people over and gaining their trust and their commitment. Every leader must speak in the language that best suits their audience if they are to achieve maximum success. Just like the Lord, who is looking at our hearts, so do the followers measure the heart of their leader.

Remarkable leaders are not motivated by money or fame, their motivation is their love for people. And their followers love them for it; some leaders will never be interviewed by *60 Minutes*, but their impact on lives will be felt forever. Simply because they have a servant's heart, great leaders will always serve their people. These leaders identify with the suffering of their people and vow to make changes. While rulers rule with their swords, leaders lead with their hearts, and the average man knows the difference. It is for this reason that no matter the mistakes that a leader makes, her people are ready to forgive her, but not a ruler, because she has shown that she does not have a heart and so her people are unforgiving towards her.

An extraordinary leader has it in her to turn ordinary women into celebrated heroes. Jael was a housewife, but when the time arose for deliverance, she stepped up to the plate and killed Sisera. A housewife turned celebrity because another woman inspired her. Distinctive leaders do not manage people but rather lead them. Managers manage to get by, but great leaders will always lead the pack. Unique leaders soar in the area that they are placed in and can produce a great amount of undeniable success stories all around them. Ordinary people become just as successful as their leader. One thing for sure is that leadership, whether good or bad, will always reproduce after their own kind. Time will tell the entire world what type of seed they were planting.

Although Deborah was a woman, it is obvious to anyone who cares to investigate that she was not only a godly leader but one who displayed proper leadership etiquette. A strong visionary, saleswoman, and a person of action, she proves that any woman can be a great leader if she so chooses. An encourager for the faint-hearted and respecter of persons, she drew out the best in people, all the while inspiring them. She understood that following God took faith and personal conviction in the face of great unrest and tribulation, thus making her a formidable champion and leader.

Chapter Two

Deborah, a Woman Born for Challenging Times!

And the children of Israel cried out to the Lord.
For Jabin had nine hundred chariots of iron, and for twenty
years he had harshly oppressed the children of Israel.
Judges 4:3

Whenever a Fortune 500 company is facing a corporate crisis, the first person they replace is the leader. They begin to seek out the best and the brightest, someone who can turn around the company. This CEO will have her background checked and verified; her accomplishments and qualifications are paraded before a board of directors, shareholders, and investors. She is hired for turbulent times, to help navigate the choppy waters of the business and change the direction of the company. In layman's terms, she is the company's last hope, and should she fail to succeed, she too will follow the same fate as her predecessor.

> ଈୠ
> **GREAT LEADERSHIP IS OFTEN TESTED AMID GREAT PROBLEMS!**
> ଈୠ

Critical times in a company call for a new person with a fresh vision to come aboard, and it was a critical time in Israel when Deborah was called to be a judge. Her calling came during the worst time in Israel's history. Having to follow in the unparalleled footsteps of Ehud, the famous great-grandson of Benjamin and of Shamgar; she found herself sandwiched between these two-great war-heroes. These were men who had attained great victories and had left behind impressive legacies. Deborah was inexperienced concerning war and had a no-name leader, so it was easy to tag her as unqualified.

As if this were not enough, she had to lead a bunch of rebellious and wayward people as well, quite a challenge for one who would be considered an outsider by those who wanted the status quo to remain the same. The fact was that the system was broken, and she represented change, a way to move forward. And this made her a moving target for those who wanted to remain in the past. She would not only have to deal with inconsistent people who had compromised their faith but was now responsible to turning them back to God. She would have to retrain them in the things of God and show them the difference between right and wrong.

Deborah was coming on board when Israel had no weaponry of any sort (Judges 5:8). Israel was militarily handicapped, and yet getting ready to war against an enemy estimated to have at least nine hundred chariots and horsemen! She had an insurmountable task of trying to rally a failing army and its faint-hearted commander, along with begging for the help of the remaining seven tribes of Israel. Sisera had iron chariots when all she had were foot soldiers.

Deborah had a crisis on her hands, a people content to remain enslaved to Jabin while lacking the faith and the military might to overcome him. It was not a great time to be a leader in Israel. She was taking the reins in a time that the good life in Israel had ceased to exist anymore.

Life was at a standstill with highways deserted and travelers avoiding their country; they were in the middle of a recession. Without the ability to trade and barter, they were in not only abject poverty but in financial ruin as well as social chaos. With no infrastructure in place, the country was suffering and on the verge of collapse. Great leadership is often tested amid great problems!

Another grueling task Deborah ahead of her was to reconcile any strained relationship that might prove to be beneficial to Israel in their time of war. One relationship that was crucial was that of the house of Heber the Kenite, which dated back to the time of Moses. Somewhere along the way, Heber was willing to side with Israel's archenemy instead of supporting them. Wise leadership understands the relevancy of historical alliances and the importance of maintaining them. Reconciliation, compromise, and peace must be an intricate part of every successful leader's agenda if one's country is to experience peace within its borders. Deborah, knowing this, had to avert the psychological implications by ensuring that everyone understood that this was their war.

Deborah knew that Israel needed as many friends as possible, and it would be up to them to make the first move. Her other strenuous task was that she lacked the military experience, background, or service record that was required for her to lead her people. She lived in a time that leaders followed their men into battle; she purposed to be no different at the request of Barak. While many might have expected her to find a reason for not taking her men into battle, she chose to go into the warfront with them. Deborah makes biblical history as the first female general who followed her troops to war, even though she had no type of experience.

Deborah had another challenging issue, which was that she was a woman! Though not directly implied here, we can be certain that her issue must have proven to be a sore topic in a time when women were not regarded as equals. It was just a few hundred years earlier did women *(namely the daughters of Zelophehad)* finally attain the constitutional rights to their father's properties in Israel. Women did not have it easy in those days, and as it should be expected, Deborah did not have many fans either because of her gender.

One of the most taxing issues that she faced in her career was Barak, the commander of the army of Israel. A man who lacked the essential leadership qualities required for an army general, he made up for his shortcomings by being obedient. Deborah would have to carry the faith and become the military strategist needed to win this war against Sisera. She would rally the faint-hearted Barak and turn him into a military hero by the time the war was over. She had no easy task galvanizing five tribes and deploying them to war with a general who was unsure of himself. Barak is remarkable as a man who refuses to allow his ego to interfere with his call to work alongside a female leader. There is one thing for sure, and that is Deborah understood that victory would not be handed over to her on a golden platter just because God hand-picked her. She would have to depend on God every step of the way; strategize and work with different types of people.

Deborah would have no past female judges' experiences or mistakes to learn from. Her leadership, whether positive or negative, would become the textbook that others would read and make future judgment calls on. She could either accept the call or hand over the responsibility to another, but she chose to press through, and the rest is history. One thing for sure is that God knew her capabilities because He had created her; things are not supposed to be easy, therefore we must learn how to move forward. There will be difficult times in which we will be criticized, made to cry and feel abandoned. But wherever we fall or fail, we must rise up again and hand over the mantle to our sons and daughters of tomorrow.

When we agree to whatever our call is, we will produce healthy young women who will know their worth and balanced young men who know how to appreciate the values of strong godly women in generations to come. God picked Deborah at Israel's lowest point in history. He was aware her gender would be put to question, and that because of it she would face great opposition. Yet none of these reasons stopped Him from choosing her, as He knew that she was also very capable. That was enough for Deborah, and surely that should hold true and be enough for anyone who is called from the household of faith.

Chapter Three

Deborah – Israel's Secret Weapon

Then Deborah said to Barak "Up! For this is the day in which the Lord has delivered Sisera into your hand. Has not the Lord gone before you? So Barak went down from Mount Tabor with ten thousand men following him
Judges 4:14

To the carnal man, picking Deborah as a spiritual leader might seem questionable. No woman had ever gone to battle, and certainly there was a place to argue about her lack of military experience. Yet inexperience did not prevent Noah from building the ark, nor is there any place for gender bias when it comes to God's work. Deborah was the edge that Israel had over Jabin, Sisera and his great army. God had decided to step outside of the box that Israel had confined Him in; she would become the new thing that He was doing.

> ଛୁଠ୍ଠ
>
> SOME OF THE GREATEST LEADERS IN TIMES PAST HAVE COME WRAPPED UP IN UNASSUMING OR UNDESIRABLE PACKAGES!
>
> ଛୁଠ୍ଠ

In a time when male leadership had failed to lead Israel into war, God chose to raise up a woman who was in tune with His voice and His perfect will. A person who could follow instructions and yet give directions that did not make sense to the ordinary man. She came on the scene with a miserable skeleton army and two-faced Israelite brethren who refused to help her win this battle. Israel needed someone fresh to bring about new life and new courage. They did not need another war hero, but a person who would become a tower of strength when everything around them was failing.

A woman who would not compromise her spiritual beliefs by yielding to the pressure of men; this helped and defined her spiritual and physical character. Compromise had become the order of the day, so God needed a person who was rock-solid in faith and could communicate with Him. Since she was a woman, neither Sisera nor Jabin would see her coming. They would underestimate her strength, they would tear her resume to pieces, they would make jest of her as a woman and wife. They would humiliate her on their circuit, but that would be fine because God had prepared something special up His sleeve concerning them. God was about to do the same thing He had done in the time of Esther, Mordecai, and Haman. While Haman was preoccupied with Mordecia, he overlooked his real threat, who was Queen Esther!

Some of the greatest leaders in times past have come wrapped up in unassuming or undesirable packages! One of the advantageous of being a woman is the power of encouragement and that people will have their guards down! Two things worked in Deborah's favor; one was that she was able to reason with Barak, the army general who had abandoned all hope of victory. Many times, women can look beyond someone façade and give them encouragement and that is what Barak needed in his life at that time. Secondly, Sisera did not believe that a woman leader would be able to take on him and his vast army. I love the movie *'**The Lord of the Rings.**'*, in the final trilogy, there stands a brave young woman who, on the battlefield, faces off with the enemy after her uncle is attacked. The enemy tells her that he cannot be killed by any man. To which she takes off her helmet and tells him that she is no man, and succeeds in killing him, ending his terror against her people.

Deborah is that woman who takes off the head of Israel's enemy and how sweet is their victory! The woman who had been miscalculated! What makes a secret weapon effective is the fact that careless mistakes are made when people underrate their opponent. There is pride involved, improper preparations, and overconfidence is seen. Whenever people misjudge their enemy, they are indirectly stating that such a person is an unworthy opponent; a person they do not view as their equal. When one is considered a formidable enemy, every precaution is taken, which also includes well-thought-out strategies and back-up plans. This honor is only given to a challenger who is worthy enough!

Since Deborah was God's secret weapon, the Lord employed other strategic plans to assist her in winning the war! What makes a secret weapon effective is the element of surprise. So you can be sure that there will be other underrated tools that will be used to help secure one's victory. The torrential rainfall of Kishon helped to cement the death of Sisera's entire army by causing their iron chariots to get stuck in the mud. He employed the elements of the weather to work in favor for the children of Israel. Rahab had flax while Deborah had the rain and Jael. Secret weapons always have with them ordinary tools to help get the job done. The *Book of Revelation* gives us spiritual insight that the final battle between God and Satan will require the assistance of a woman called the Church. Any war general who has refused to investigate and learn from history's successes and failures will never be adequately prepared for war.

Every general must understand the people she seeks to fight, understand their terrain, their language, and culture, but most of all their spiritual belief. History has proven time and time again that war is not necessarily won by military might or technological gadgets. Men will grow weary, technology will fail, but one's faith will outlast any weapon or abilities. Leaders who fall short of learning these important lessons will meet defeat, like *Alexander the Great*, who was one of the greatest war heroes who ever lived but died from the bite of a mosquito.

Whether it is the pirates of Somalia or the rough and hampering terrain of Afghanistan; soldiers must understand the religion of their opponents and master their terrain to win. A secret weapon is like playing cards, when called upon to play your last hand. Your opponent does not know your card. He looks out for a sign, something that will give him a clue. God holds all the cards in His hands, and no one knows which one He is playing: a female judge, heavy rainfall, or His final card, a friendly housewife called Jael, who used an everyday house tool to gain the victory for Israel.

Sadly, those who underestimated Deborah as a secret weapon paid dearly for it by falling into the unexpected hands of God's final plan, called Jael. The question begs if you will agree to be God's secret weapon. You are only as effective as the tool that is in your hands.

Chapter Four

Deborah, a Benefit to Her People

Village life had ceased, it ceased in Israel. Until I, Deborah, arose. Arose a mother in Israel... Judges 5:7

While the story of Deborah shows how God can use an ill-equipped army and a female general to produce victory; we tend to forget that Deborah had a day job as a judge. Her responsibility was to judge matters judiciously. Judging required careful mediation while using one's authority in a godly manner. A gift, no doubt, that God had entrusted her with, along with a prophetic eye, must have only enhanced her abilities. With this placed squarely upon her shoulder, we can see that she must have tempered the law with compassion.

> ೫०ೞ
>
> GREAT LEADERS FIGHT WAR ON THEIR OWN TERMS AND IN THEIR OWN TERRAIN, THUS PLACING THEM IN AN ADVANTAGEOUS POSITION.
>
> ೩०ೕ

A fair leader is a woman who understands how to juggle judgment and compassion simultaneously, thus making her a benefit to her people. You can tell a leader's worth by how they immediately spring into action when everything around them is at a standstill! Deborah was extremely profitable to Israel because she did not wait for something to happen; she made things happen! She refused to wait for war to find her; she readily initiated the battle against Sisera on her own terms. Great leaders fight war on their own terms and in their own terrain, thus placing them in an advantageous position.

Since it was Deborah who was leading Israel, it was up to her to decide the direction of the war. She used the home-front advantage against Sisera and his army by instructing Barak and his troops to go to Mount Tabor while Sisera's army got trapped at River Kishon. She knew every corner and crevice of her land along with God, who strategically led her enemies to a muddy battleground. This woman knew that winning the war would also mean using the terrain around her wisely.

How unfortunate that many of today's women are waiting on others to validate their call or are operating outside of it. Wherever your call is, you have a home field advantage that you need to use. The same principle is applied in the NFL, whereby the home team playing ought to have the advantage over the guest team in the house! Deborah worked offensively rather than defensively to gain meaningful results for her people. Great leaders must marry wisely. Regrettably, this has become too familiar an issue in the kingdom of God today: inflexible and competitive spouses seeking to destroy the agenda of God.

I believe that she allowed God to pick her husband, thus she married a very secure man called Lapidoth, who allowed her the liberty to juggle marriage, ministry, and career together. While many of her male counterparts struggled in this area, she seemed to flourish. Deborah's uniqueness had her married to an extraordinary man, a husband secured in himself and his wife's calling. He was her greatest supporter as he assisted her in fulfilling the call of God upon her life. Sensing the greatness in his wife, he chose to work behind the scenes instead of being in the limelight. He never asked her to choose between ministry and marriage, silencing her critics by proving that it was possible to have the best of both worlds if married to a flexible spouse.

Yes, ministry and marriage can co-exist side by side, which was the original plan in the Garden of Eden! The Church today would be much stronger if up-and-coming single female leaders would just allow God to pick their husbands. Secure men never trample or deny their wives their own visions but help nurture and uphold them. Lapidoth knew that Israel needed a capable leader, and what an honor it was for him to be married to such a woman. A secure female leader needs to have a confident spouse who understands what she is all about. A great leader's gift will make room for her and attract other like-minded people to her.

Gifts are meant to positively impact the lives of others. A woman who has a gift will cause her to stand out from among the crowd; it will get her noticed by the right people who can help foster and harness that gift. It also causes everyone to seek that woman out. Our gift in the right locations will challenge people and cause us to reign triumphantly. Your gift has a location that it is meant to prosper in, and failure to walk in it will compromise the people you claim to love and serve. Great leaders have great gifts. Deborah's gift supported, serviced, and comforted all who needed it. She was beneficial to her country in a time when everything was chaotic. God raised her up to reassure the downtrodden and to console the brokenhearted. Answering one's call makes that leader discover her other hidden talents that translate into areas of strength and abilities.

Deborah was more than just a judge and a war heroine but became the voice of women everywhere in the kingdom. She becomes the primary example of what every woman can achieve if she discovers her path of destiny. By her discovering her area of service, Deborah becomes the inspiration for all women in Israel, the young and old, the housewives to career women, the married and single. She is not just a benefit to her people, but also to her gender! She gives them the encouragement to find their place in the kingdom. A woman leader must realize that she shoulders a greater responsibility to not only mankind, but to her fellow women as well.

Where there is a calling, it also means that others have either failed or God has created an opportunity for a revival. For any leader to be beneficial to her people, she needs to examine, repair, and overhaul the system that has been broken. God strategically placed Deborah in the position of judge to correct the system from inside out, a concept that rogue ministers fail to understand. To be valuable in a community, there are two major questions that must be answered, and they are who your audience is and what type of service are you providing to them? Good leaders provide exceptional service to their people. The leader who can provide her people with a profitable environment, a safe community, and a productive lifestyle is a leader many people will follow.

Deborah understood that people needed someone to believe in including the availability of human services and economic empowerment. Since she was cognizant of is theory, she worked it to her advantage. A good leader is called upon to break down historical and unfair stereotyping of her abilities. Great leaders change people's perception about them by accomplishing the supernatural. Women who are bent on becoming the best leaders must allow God to use them outside of the box. Being typical and practical sometimes must be done away with, if you want to embrace the unexpected! There are many times that breaking away from the norm will lead to a season of the extraordinary.

If no woman has achieved what you are about to do, the reason is that it is God's timing to do so. He made and called you to handle the demands of that job, ministry, or household. Gender bias is not an acceptable excuse any more than height, education, or background. Locate your dominant gift, as there lies your ministry. Sit under that palm tree that has your name attached to it, because in the fullness of time you will become indispensable and of service to the people who need you the most, Israel.

Chapter Five

Deborah the Worshiper

The song of Deborah
Then Deborah and Barak the son of Abinoam sang on that day,
saying. Hear O kings! Give ear, O princes! I, even I will sing to the
Lord; I will sing praises to the Lord God of Israel
Judges 5:1, 3

Deborah was a woman of worship! One out of the two chapters dedicated to her had her singing a song of victory in the entire chapter, while the first one just summed up all her achievements! Apart from being the only female judge of her time, Deborah stands out from among the rest of the judges as a chief worshipper in her own rights. None of her counterparts can compare to her when it comes to worship, a woman who knew how to intimately touch God through her worship. True worshippers do not use empty words to entice God; worship is a heart-moving and life-changing experience for them. It is a place of sincere praise.

> ℘↺ଔ
>
> WORSHIP
> MUST
> PERMEATE
> EVERY AREA OF
> OUR LIVES
> PHYSICALLY,
> EMOTIONALLY,
> FINANCIALLY,
> MATRIMONIALLY
> AND
> SPIRITUALLY
>
> ଔ↺℘

Worshippers are not people-pleasers, nor are their praise momentary, but they are people desiring spiritual intimacy with God. Deborah might have been a wife, a prophetess, a military strategist, and a judge, but she was first and foremost a worshipper. A woman in love with God! The true measure of any great spiritual leader can be discovered in her worship.

Every spiritual leader in the Bible had a special reservation for worship in their lives for God, and she was no different. Worship plays a vital role in ministry and holds a significant meaning especially in times of war. Mary, the mother of Jesus Christ, prophetically coined a song when she had conceived by the Holy Ghost. And in the Book of Revelation, we are introduced to innumerable angels and the elders worshipping God. Worship should be an intricate integral part of any great spiritual leader; and Deborah had a heart of worship. Worship is a sign of unprecedented devotion to the Lord, and Deborah was devoted.

She honored His commandment, proving that worship remains today the highest form of prayer. True worshippers are not just truthful beings but spiritual ones as well. They are instruments of music; thus, worship comes to them easily and effortlessly. Since worship is tied to our love for God, it should come naturally to us as it did for Deborah. In her worship, she tells the story of God's awesome victory against His enemies just as in the time of Miriam, the sister of Moses. Worship is an open invitation to devote oneself to the Lord. Her song to the Lord spiritually and physically stirred up the people of God.

Today, we would call it political awareness or communal issues being told through the avenue of music. Though to many this type of music seems like a new phenomenon, it has its roots in ancient and biblical history. Her worship addressed the societal ills of the land, but also described what proper leadership should resemble. Though her song speaks of Israel's suffering, pain, and betrayal of its sisterly tribes, it also talks about the joy of God winning the war and defeating the enemy by the hands of an unlikely woman. She ends her worship by illustrating that those who love Him will be like the shining sun!

Her adoration for God radiates through her song; aware that without God there could be no victory whatsoever. She knows that worship transcends beyond the borders of gender, language, and skin color. She knows that true worship melts the hardest of hearts and builds a bridge of unity where there was none. She knows that worship is more than mere words, but an act of unbridled affection for God, in which one cannot exist without each other. If godly women are to take their place in these last days, we must mirror the worshipping lifestyle of Deborah, carrying it beyond the confines of our pulpits into every crack and crevice of our lives.

Worship must permeate every area of our lives physically, emotionally, financially, matrimonially, and spiritually. There should be no room made for games or gimmicks. Our worship life is meant to be so life-changing that ministers and congregants alike should be unable to withstand His glory when He is truly revered. Authentic worship produces authentic results, fulfills every human need, and lifts us up to unusual places of influence when our worship is well-pleasing.

Real worship is a two-way street between man and God; ever intertwining us closer to our Maker. Let us hold fast to our worship, and in the famous words of Christ Jesus to the woman He met at the well: *"Those that worship God must do so in spirit and in truth."* A sign that you are a worshipper is that both God's truth and spirit is found inside of you.

Chapter Six

Deborah – The Multi-Tasker

Now Deborah, a prophetess, the wife of Lapidoth was judging Israel at that time. And she would sit under the palm tree of Deborah between Ramah and Bethel in the mountains of Ephraim. And the children of Israel came up to her for judgment
Judges 4: 4-5

While every leader has a special skill or talent that makes them unique, to lead all must perfect the art of multitasking. And Deborah was great at multitasking; she was a minister, judge, wife, encourager, and a military strategist. The leader who can manage several things effectively at one time will always be ahead of her peers. Today's woman is no different from Deborah, who must run her family, the office, the church and yet partake in other social activities, all the while allowing little or no room for mistakes. We are first introduced to Deborah as a prophetess and a wife all in the same sentence, proving that ministry and marriage can be intertwined together.

As a prophetess, she becomes the mouthpiece of God for her people, directing and guiding them into a time of war that would eventually produce peace in their land. Her prophetic office helps her as a leader by affording her the insight to see hidden gifts in others that will work in conjunction with God's agenda. A good leader allows God to introduce her, and not men. As the Lapidoth's wife, we

> ಬಂಡ
> **A BAD LEADER MAKES IMPORTANT DECISIONS BY PLAYING THINGS BY EAR WHILE A GOOD LEADER IS ALWAYS ADEQUATELY EQUIPPED WITH A STRATEGY.**
> ಬಂಡ

know that Deborah must also handle the responsibilities of marriage as well. She balances the demands of ministry, marriage, and work well.

For her to be successful, it will require the help of her husband to make things easier for her. Lapidoth is the type of husband who is far ahead of his contemporaries in his ability to assist his wife when works make certain demands of her. He is a true testimony to the fact that a woman can have it all if she has the loving support of her husband. Lapidoth, which means *'torch,'* must have been the light shining ever so brightly in Deborah's most trying times. He must have been dependable and stable; his silent strength is seen through the leadership qualities of his wife. Deborah never loses sight of the fact that she must fulfill the expectations of a wife and does so gladly.

Apart from being a prophetess and wife, she also worked as a judge, handling a variety of issues that people brought to her. She had to temper every judgment with the law, knowledge, discernment, and wisdom. As a judge, she was responsible for keeping people's confidence and making the difficult decisions. To be a great leader, people must know that you will keep their confidence and trust enough that you can make the tough calls. A good leader must always judge every situation according and wisely. Deborah describes herself as a mother in Israel, letting us knows that she was looked upon as a mother to many.

While there is no record of her having children of her own, it did not erase the motherly instinct that she carried within her. And had she been a mother, she definitely would not have been the typical type who would bake her children's cookies and wave them off at the doorstep as they went off to school.

Deborah would have made for a great mother, but it might have been her husband making the cookies while she brought home the milk after work. A good leader who multitasks must learn how to ask her spouse for help so that she is not overstretched in the home. With a supportive husband and understanding children, she can accomplish the unimaginative. As a great leader, this type of woman will never be your typical wife or mother, and that is okay. There are other tasks that we fulfill as people that might not have typical titles like mother or judge, and one of them for Deborah was that of an encourager. A great leader must inspire others to follow her through encouraging words and actions.

Deborah the leader invokes the spirit of patriotism and unity in a people who had already lost hope. She changed the mindset of ten thousand men from slavery to victory. On a separate note, Deborah was successful in engineering and building strategic relationships between men and women as a team. A great leader brings about equilibrium to the male-female relationship in the workplace. She did not have to compromise her womanhood to produce harmony in the kingdom. She understood the power of diplomacy, making sure she was not a threat to men while at the same empowering a new generation of women. The art of negotiation wins to your side your worse critics. Deborah knew that she would have to win both men and women who believed in the traditional views that a woman's place was only in the home.

This exceptional leader recognized that harsh words do not win your decriers over but rather tact and tolerance can work wonders. For any woman to become a great leader, she must cultivate the art of diplomacy in an ever-changing and hostile world. Speaking your mind every time will make you lose out on opportunities for team building and successful alliances. Deborah is a great strategic military advisor, a role that she handles well. Every good leader must have a strategy by which she can implement her vision. While she is unable to handle a sword, she is seasoned enough to hear from God on how to methodically defeat the Canaanite army.

She strategically directs Barak on where to gather his troops to maximize their position and ensure precise execution of her plan against the enemy. She is a woman with an angle and a sure approach. The divine direction of God for the war ensures complete success. Without a plan, a leader will experience failure. A bad leader makes important decisions by playing things by ear while a good leader is always adequately equipped with a strategy. Deborah was many things: a wife, judge, prophetess, woman, encourager, diplomat, and strategist.

She handled every role with dignity no matter how challenging it proved to be. In some instances, her role was clearly defined, while other times there were no line of demarcation. Since she was great at multitasking, she avoided being stereotyped or pigeon-holed. As incredible as she might have been, Deborah shared her credit with her husband and the men and women who assisted her in the most difficult times in Israel. A great leader is always reinventing herself; never allowing the world to define who she is as a woman and a leader.

She is the ultimate woman, who puts out fires on the job, cooks dinner on arriving home, helps her children with their homework, and takes care of her husband. This woman does the task of many and yet is still able to produce a desirable result. A great leader produces in whatever role she might find herself. Today, you might be unappreciated for all the multi-tasking that you are doing, but if you faint not and allow the Lord to perfect you, in due season God will cause the world to recognize you.

Chapter Seven

Prophetess Deborah – The Gift of God

'Go and deploy troops at Mount Tabor, take with you ten thousand men of sons of Naphtali and the sons of Zebulun, and against you I will deploy Sisera, the commander of Jabin's army with his chariots and his multitude at the River Kishon and I will deliver him into your hands?"
Judges 4:7

A good leader operates within her God-given office. Deborah was the prophetic voice for her time, a gift accompanied by the spirit of discernment, word of knowledge, and wisdom. A gift that must be handled responsibly and whenever Israel sinned in the past; the gift of prophecy would become extinct. No word in the land meant a lack of direction, signifying the advancement of impeding and certain destruction.

> ౭౦౮
>
> A GIFTED LEADER PROVOKES ORDINARY PEOPLE INTO DOING EXTRAORDINARY THINGS AND AIDS THEM IN DISCOVERING THEIR PURPOSE!
>
> ౭౦౮

The death of Moses saw the end of the prophetic move of God in Israel until the introduction of Deborah. God was not just bringing back this office but also bringing back order to His kingdom! A prophetic leader understands that her gift is to be used to help God's people! A gift is a present, reward or endowment of some sort to a person who is either deserving of it or in need of some sort, and even though Israel was undeserving of His gift, God decided to give them a prophetic gift called Deborah.

Her job was not just to win the war, but to win back the heart of the people to God. A true prophetess turns people in the direction of God instead of fulfilling her own selfish agenda. Deborah demonstrated that she was the woman for the job as she was bent on leading God's people down the path of repentance and behavior modification. Prophetic leaders understand that without repentance there can be no spiritual or physical transformation.

Deborah would have to become the people's conscience, because the rebellious have no fear or remorse. She would have to retrain them in the way of God and His word. A prophetic leader understands that she has a tough assignment and that not everyone can be won. Her mission did not guarantee that everyone would agree with her or accept her as a gift of God. Every (true) prophet struggles with the rejection of her people. She understood that not everyone would accept the word of God from her, nor would they respect her calling. A prophetess must be ready to suffer for the call.

Deborah understood that she had to complete her mission whether it be with a few or many. She had to accept the fact that many would not receive her, such as the tribes that had refused to fight alongside them, or Barak's refusal in facing Sisera alone. A prophetic leader must learn not to take things personally. Deborah learned early that people's rejection of her was a rejection of God. This simply means that even if you are an expert, there are Christians who will justify through empty reasoning why they are disobeying God. She learned early not to cast her pearls before swine. Every prophetess is called to address a particular condition in a specific location. Anyone who operates outside their location will never be fully functional.

Deborah stayed within the borders of her calling and her location; she did not attempt to rule outside of her God-given domain. The condition of Israel was moral decay and slavery, and God had raised her up to get rid of them. She was not confused about her call, nor was she everywhere. A good leader knows when there is something unique about her gift. It was the distinctiveness of her gift that helped defeat Israel's twenty-year old enemy. The contribution of one's gift can easily change the outcome of a terrible situation to a favorable one. Deborah was that gift.

Every prophetic leader knows that her gift will compensate her. Real prophetesses do not sell their gifts for profit or personal gain. The fact is compensation comes in many different forms: finance, health, marriage, peace, or even a successful ministry. An honorable minister will never seek for fame, knowing that God is her just prize. God in turn views her faithful and then rewards her accordingly and not before she has proven herself. A prophetic leader must be ready to pay the price for her gift. Deborah understood that her gift would not shield her from disappointments or betrayals. Seven of the twelve tribes of Israel disappointed her and so did Heber by siding with Sisera. What did she do? She continued forward, and that is what a great leader does.

Great leaders know when they need to take a step back, regroup, and continue. A prophetic leader uses her setback to stage a comeback. Deborah could have been disillusioned by what she saw around her, but instead she focused on her skeleton army, the support of her husband, and her God! She readied herself to work with those who were available and did not wait for the experts. A great prophetic leader is the woman who can work with people who have shortcomings. Deborah was no different. She had to coach a faithless general and inspired a housewife who had no military training!

A good leader learns to improvise and so Deborah was forced to employ the help of a few men to win the war. This did not deter her but made her stronger, sharpened her gift only for the better. A prophetic leader seals her victory by the words that she speaks. Deborah prophesied how the war would be won. Those who refuse to assist her in executing the will of God will find out that they are dispensable after all. He will replace them on the battlefield with someone who lacks their expertise and training. A prophetic gift moves the people of God forward. Deborah's gift advanced her people in every area, from slavery to liberty, from a nation of irrelevancy to one of great importance. Everything she touched bore fruits of significance.

Good leadership facilitates change, but great leadership ignites a movement. Deborah was a great leader because once she started motivating her people; it picked up momentum. Wherever there is a cause, gifts will be discovered; wherever there is inspiration God will invoke a crusade or movement. Deborah's gift returned hope to her people and caused them to believe once again, giving them the necessary drive to make things happen to change their lives. A gifted leader provokes ordinary people into doing extraordinary things and aids them in discovering their purpose!

Deborah's unique gift made ordinary people want to get involved. The unknown tribes of Zebulun and Naphtali were suddenly thrust into the limelight for their fighting skills, an honor that had once been reserved only for the warring tribes of Benjamin and Judah. Suddenly the underdogs in a society are given a chance at national recognition and fame; the gift of one person can move them from a nonentity to somebody and from obscurity to popularity. She created an opportunity for nameless tribes to be renowned and for women nationwide to become fascinated and involved in saving their country. A talented leader captivates the lost and the rejected of a society and gives them purpose. Deborah was a dangerous leader because she got the rejected and the despised of Israel to discover their hidden talents and untapped gifts within them.

She made them relevant; Barak became spellbound; the tribes Naphtali and Zebulun were awestruck; women were mesmerized enough to provoke Jael into becoming a risk taker! All these reactions were made possible because she had offered herself as a gift to God, and in turn they offered their gifts to their nation Israel. A brilliant leader helps her people to discover the use of their gifting and locate their passions that they are unaware of. Barak and Jael are proof that the gift of one person can provoke the gift of greatness in one another. A capable leader walks in the power of her gifting.

Deborah recognized that where there is authorization, there is also direction. Every form of power comes with instructions to bring about productivity. From Barak the general to Jael the housewife, each person involved had the license to make a difference in their nation, and they did. No matter the brilliance of a leader, there are certain times when things are simply out of her hands. Deborah had done all that she could to ensure the victory of Israel on the field, Sisera had escaped on foot, routed by God into the tent of Jael. All that Deborah knew was that Sisera would be killed by the hands of a woman, but God did not give her the entire master plan. In the end, a prophetic leader must realize that God can do the unexpected so that no one person takes His glory.

The day ended the way that God planned, and every prophetic leader must understand what is most important which is the victory and not who God uses to deliver it. A prophetic leader must realize that her gift has a variety of components attached to it and it is her responsibility to discover the different ways that God wants to use it. She must learn to nurture and build it, refuse to abuse it but wisely use it. It is not her personal gift but one that God has entrusted to her care for service when He has need of it for His people. She must remember, like the people, she is undeserving of it and that is why it is by grace.

A gift's relevancy is determined by its owner and what she chooses to do with it, remembering that she will be held accountable. Deborah, God's gift to Israel, followed instructions, encouraged Barak, and engineered the death of Sisera by a homemaker. What powerful things we can accomplish whenever we allow ourselves to be used as a gift for God and for His kingdom!

Chapter Eight

Deborah – A Woman in the Right Position!

And the princes of Issachar were with Deborah as Issachar so was Barak. Sent into the valley under his command, among the divisions of Reuben. There was great resolves of heart
Judges 5:15

A good leader will remain in her rightful position. The people of Israel were about to experience great joy because Deborah was a woman who was in her rightful position. She was at the right place during the right time, accomplishing the right things. Her position afforded her the opportunity to help the less fortunate. A bad leader abuses her position; using it for profit or to mistreat the disadvantaged. Divine positioning comes from Lord, created by a crisis, merit, or purpose.

> ℰℐℂℛ
>
> **WEAK LEADERS CRUMBLE UNDER PRESSURE WHILE GREAT LEADERS EXCEL, RARELY EXPERIENCING ANY TYPE OF FAILURE!**
>
> ℰℐℂℛ

He placed her there to gain His people back, change discriminatory mindsets, and restore peace and glory to Israel. Weak leaders crumble under pressure while great leaders excel, rarely experiencing any type of failure! A crisis is one of the greatest tools of assessing one's position in a business, ministry, and relationship, and Deborah stood out, separating her from the rest of the leaders that were in Israel.

When others complained, she sought out for solutions; when tribes bailed, she gathered the remnant and moved forward. She positioned herself mentally, and it was seen in the way she attacked the crisis of her nation with precision and great confidence. A good leader positions herself advantageously to get great things done. And this she did very well as she used diplomacy while working tenaciously. As both spiritual head and judge of Israel, she had to topple their slavery mindset and prepare them for liberty, no easy task for any leader. She had to use her rank as leader to get the entire country to buy into her vision of change, while chipping away at their fearful perception of war.

It takes a great leader to change the mindset of a disenchanted nation, and Deborah would have to use her position to do it. Amid tragedy, a fearful leader will abandon her God-given position. Deborah had an additional crisis on her hands, which was Barak wanting to give up his status as Israel's general. The lack of resources has many times determined the loyalty of a man, and Barak was no different. Through the avenue of love and encouragement, Deborah gently convinced him to remain in position.

An effective leader uses her position to gain correct information. Wrong information will produce wrong results, and Deborah knew this; once Barak was back in position, she rightly ascertained the tribes who would support them in battle and those who refused. Even though God had assured victory, she did not want to go to war with the wrong type of people. She needed men who would not break rank and could follow the commands of a woman, putting aside their personal emotions or sentiments to get the work done. She did not just need Barak but also 10,000 who were in the right place. A good leader will be tested by one person who seems to be weak but who can turn around through encouragement. Deborah was in a sticky situation with Barak, who lacked strength and commitment at Israel's most critical time.

While he failed to display any great leadership qualities, he honored Deborah's invitation to meet. It is a risk that a leader must take when team-members might suggest getting rid of essential supportive leaders who fall below their expectations. She must have the trained eye of an eagle to see far into Barak's future. A well-positioned leader sometimes gives an opportunity to people whom others have written off. Deborah saw beyond Barak's weakness, that he was a man would fight a well-equipped enemy army without adequate weaponry for his own soldiers.

A well-placed leader, who can inspire men, can undoubtedly do the same for women. When Deborah was able to rally Barak and his men into position, the women also found their place. She had to find an approach that would gain her an audience with the women. It had to be tailored specifically to her gender. A good leader finds what works for her and will turn it into a workable process; she must appeal to the mothers, aunts, sisters, housewives, and working mothers to get them on her side. A good leader must be able to relate and speak the language of her people. A good leader must have the right platform in which to deliver her vision. Deborah had to come across to the women as their friend and not barking orders. She had to be inspirational and yet revolutionary by encouraging women to do whatever was necessary.

As well-positioned leader, she provoked women from the workforce to the home-front to secure Israel's future and that of their children. Her message must have been clear and concise that if she could risk her life, she needed them to do the same. When she won Barak over, she also motivated the nation's women to think beyond their gender and act for the betterment of their families and themselves. A good leader knows that every battle is determined by the leader's attitude and behavior. Deborah's position did not define her, nor did it hamper her attitude.

While opposition and disappointment come with leadership, every leader must cultivate 'a poker face' when others have given up. The unexpected will happen while in leadership, but it is not the time or the reason to give up. Deborah did not wait for the war to arrive at her doorsteps, but with the attitude of a winner, she changed the direction of the war. There are people in every leader's team who will disappoint you, but that should not be enough to throw you off course. Secure your attitude, get your game face, and determine that you will win and not lose, that is what Deborah did! A well-positioned leader must understand that distraction will lead to destruction, so she must learn to remain focused. Deborah knew it was time for war and so she was not busy judging or making dinner. Sadly, there are so many leaders who focus on the wrong things and then wonder why they keep failing.

A good leader knows her priorities, while a bad leader will suffer massive casualty. Deborah's main concern was winning the war, which took front stage to everything else in her life, including judging, prophesying, and her marriage. She realized that if she broke her focus, she would be jobless, without a ministry and a marriage. By going to war, she was securing not just her family, but everything that mattered to her. A good leader will always have to make tough choices. Deborah was no different; should she follow her troop to war? What about her husband, her ministry, and her job? No woman had done what she was embarking on and was it foolish of her?

Great leaders do not always have all the answers, but they do the best with what they have been given. At the end of the day, Deborah made the right call by supporting her army and securing Israel its well needed victory. She not only had a country to return to, but a family, a ministry, and a job, along with peace. When you prioritize the right things in your life, you will find great success. God placed Deborah in the most powerful and coveted position attainable in Israel as its leader; using her position to effectively bring about change that benefited everyone.

Her radical moves brought recognition to the tribes of Zebulun and Naphtali, while proving through Barak and Jael that men and women could work as a team. She single-handedly gave the ordinary woman an opportunity to shine by tapping into her unused gifts. Everyone can rise to the occasion when the right woman allows God to put her in her rightful position!

Chapter Nine

Deborah – An Empowered Woman

Then Deborah arose and went with Barak to Kedesh. And Barak called Zebulun and Naphtali to Kedesh; he went up with ten thousand men under his command and Deborah went up with him

Judges 4: 9-10

A powerful leader is that woman who makes great things happen. Deborah was such a woman, and because of her influence she was able to reach out to the ordinary people. It is a wise leader who knows that power comes in many different forms, and Deborah used every type that was made available to her. She used her influence as a married woman to rally the married women into action. Many could relate to the wife and career woman that she presented to the public. While the men saw her as a wife accountable to her husband, the women realized that being married did not prevent them from positively impacting their nation.

> ෨෬
>
> A GOOD LEADER MUST NOT DISPLAY SIGNS OF INCONSISTENCY, AS HER PEOPLE WILL VIEW IT AS A FORM OF WEAKNESS.
>
> ෨෬

An influential leader can better influence those who look like her! An empowered leader understands the law and adheres to it. Deborah must have been chosen by God because of her ability to operate within the confines of the law and remain impartial and merciful when handing out judgments. A good leader has the power of persuasion at her fingertips. Deborah could not have achieved the level of success that she did without it, especially in the tough economic climate that she found herself in.

Every gift she had was used to help Israel. A good leader must not display signs of inconsistency, as her people will view it as a form of weakness. Deborah never cracked under pressure, and if she had her moments, perhaps only her husband saw them. Her people had to believe in what she believed, and any sign of weakness would have left people discouraged.

An empowered leader must be a compelling one. The power of Deborah is seen by her ability to win over Barak in joining her to fight against Sisera. She was able to convince the army general to meet her on her own terms in a time when women had no influence or even a voice. A powerful leader must be a credible one, able to win her toughest critics to her side, and this was what Deborah was able to do.

Such leaders want to win, and so by sheer determination they ensure that they get the necessary swing votes of key people. It is paramount for a powerful leader to build the right type of team from the beginning. Deborah knew that she needed a winning team and that she needed certain men who would validate her position concerning the war. Who better than an army general, even if she had to force him out of retirement! While she won him on her own terms, she also learned that she had to bend a little to achieve her goal. Great leaders bend a little when there is too much at stake, and they want to win.

A great leader must also be a great orator. One of Deborah's undeniable attributes was that she was an eloquent speaker. The leader who fails to articulate her message effectively will always lose out to the one who can speak brilliantly. Esther's speech moved her husband, and her life and the lives of her people were spared. Abigail's words swayed the angry David in showing mercy to her household. Deborah's poetic ability resonates from her song of praise to the Lord after attaining victory, displaying her worshiper side, but that is not enough. She must have been a powerhouse of a speaker to rally a homemaker into making her believe that she was somebody great.

An illustrious leader can speak to the treasure buried inside of the everyday woman. An empowered leader will never embrace failure as an option. Deborah had the knack to speak to the forgotten and unite them to fight a war that looked humanly impossible to win. An eloquent speaker finds the hidden giants within the timid and releases them into their destiny, and she did just that! Effective communication is what every good leader must develop, and she must know her audience. When Deborah spoke to Barak, she addressed him as a general and not a failure. In talking to the masses, she must have spoken with the spirit of patriotism, and yet when reaching out to her gender, she used the language of a mother, wife, daughter, and sister.

Deborah used a different presentation for different audiences. A remarkable leader is one who has a strong sense of conviction. It is this passion that drives them in all that they do, and Deborah was a woman of great conviction and faith. While others sleep, she remains awake until she finds a solution. No matter the odds against her, a weaponless army, an unstable general, a novice army, and the betrayal of sisterly tribes would daunt the faith of other leaders, but these challenges only fueled it.

An extraordinary leader does not fold when a door suddenly closes; she breaks through the window instead! Once you understand their passion, you are given the choice to join or disassociate from them. An incredible leader needs no convincing; just point her in the direction of her enemy. Since Deborah knew that the war was winnable, she had no problem following Barak to the battlefield. After all, what was a little bit of dirt compared to ending twenty years of slavery! An outstanding leader has one responsibility which is to get the job done! This explains why she is so electrifying and has such a presence in any event that she graces.

The best leader is the one who has been underestimated. If Sisera thought that Deborah would back down because she was a woman, understaffed and weaponless, he must have been sorely disappointed. Every doubt was dispelled when she went with her troops to confront him! A great leader who is way ahead of her time will always make for a formidable opponent! And Deborah was just that, a woman ahead of her generation and peers. A married female general on a battlefield was totally unheard of for that time. A great leader must know her limitations. With all the gifts that she had, Deborah did not know how to handle a sword and left the fighting for Barak to do.

As a leader, she recognized her strength and used it, and knew when to let others step in. How sad it is that so many leaders want to do everything and then conveniently blame Satan when they fail to succeed! She was a judge, and he was a warrior and she allowed him to excel in his gift and did not interfere with it! A good leader keeps her vision simple for it to be attainable. What made Deborah powerful was her ability to keep things simple and to the minimum. Throughout the history of Israel, God had always used few to attain His will, and she understood that it was not all about numbers but the people's heart. So, Deborah never crumbles under the first sign of trouble, but she resolved every issue wisely.

Good leaders never discard profitable relationships. She proved this point by working closely with Barak the general. Deborah displayed an aptitude for reconciliation and team building, two important components in leadership. Mistakes made only make the team stronger and better. As Israel's leader, she kept things simple, and so did the people around her. A terrific leader has the power to influence others in recognizing their own strengths. Deborah used her office as a woman to advance the causes of the women in her nation, giving them a voice. She was dissatisfied being the only woman at the table and helped birth the likes of Jael to share the same platform with her.

She wanted Israel "empowered" but quickly recognized that if women remained silent that the world would be denied their great contributions of excellence. Until gender bias ended, Deborah would have to become the beacon of hope for all women, knowing that gender has nothing to do with being a great leader. She was exceptional because she paved the way for others of her kind to walk through and make a visible difference. Hopefully, today's spiritual leaders globally will begin to share their authentic experiences with the next upcoming generations as the corporate world does in building great leaders of tomorrow.

So many churches leaders are guilty of holding back tomorrow's leaders from reaching their full potential, out of jealousy and personal insecurities. This leaves many people broken, rejected, and frustrated. A good leader pays the price so that her people do not have to! God empowers a leader so that she can empower someone less fortunate than her. Deborah was irrefutably one of Israel's greatest leaders; she knew how to capitalize on people's strengths by helping them discover their hidden talents. She taught the world that a woman could be a brilliant military strategist and a successful career woman, while Jael learned that power can also be found in the hands of a housewife. Ultimately, when power is evenly distributed among ordinary people, success becomes visible, and this is true power actualized.

Chapter Ten

Deborah – A Woman of Great Boldness

*Zebulun is a people who jeopardized their lives to the point of
death, Naphtali also, on the heights of the battlefield
Judges 5:18*

> ❧ℭℛ
>
> **THERE IS A DIFFERENCE BETWEEN A RISK-TAKING LEADER AND A RECKLESS LEADER. A RISK TAKER IS MOTIVATED BY PEOPLE AND THE MISSION, WHILE THE RECKLESS IS MOTIVATED BY SELF-GRATIFICATION, GREED, AND FAME.**
>
> ❧ℭℛ

Courageous leader thrives in any environment! Deborah stands as the undisputed heavyweight champion of female biblical leaders, willing to enter a male-dominated arena and still managing to come out on top. She needed to be bold for what she was up against; a broken-down system, gender bias, a nation of rebels, a bankrupt economy, a weaponless army, and an unavoidable war were just the beginning of Israel's problems!

While men's hearts were failing, hers was singing songs of victory. Not to be intimidated by these reports, she marches into battle with a skeleton army, going boldly where no woman has gone before, to wage war! Great leaders are a rare breed. And so was she, a woman with a strong backbone and resilience to match. Deborah accomplishes so much: she holds down a job, establishes a ministry, goes to war, and runs her household! Assertive leaders pave the way for other bold people to follow. She was a master at building confidence in others as a leader, knowing that good leadership requires becoming adventurous.

Every great leader must become a risk taker to reach their divine purpose, and Deborah was one! She gambled on Barak while weighing the consequences of using Zebulun and Naphtali as a secondary army. But she took that chance anyway and won! Fearful leaders step back while audacious leaders lunge forward! When the seven tribes of Israel had given up, Deborah along with five others launched forward. I have often heard people say that when God could not locate a man to fight against Sisera, He chose Deborah. I disagree with that theory; God chose Deborah because she was QUALIFIED! When Barak was unwilling to take the initial risk, He chose a homemaker to help secure Israel's victory to send a message that all women matter.

The courageous leader must exercise self-discipline! Deborah and Jael exhibited true restraint of character, an admirable quality, as risk takers seek out the best interests of the group while selfish leaders think of only themselves. There is a difference between a risk-taking leader and a reckless leader. A risk taker is motivated by people and the mission, while a reckless one is motivated by self-gratification, greed, and fame. Jael was a risk taker, waiting for the perfect opportunity to kill Sisera.

Jael was able to exhibit total self-control because she had a leader who exemplified the same traits.

Deborah was that self-assured leader with razor focus and Jael showed similar signs of leadership by keeping her emotions under control when she had to face Sisera alone. Level-headedness is what is most needed when all the chips are down, and such a person will always be respected by her peers and experts alike. While Jael may not have been an army general, the entire country owed her a debt of gratitude because of her composure at Israel's most critical time.

Every good leader will have their character examined in a time of trouble. A woman is judged by the storms that she can weather, and Deborah was no exception. A leader's reputation is either broken or established in such the toughest of seasons. Her character as a leader was tested before the court of public opinions as thousands waited to see if she would crack under the pressure. Instead, she rose above her critics, proving to everyone that God had chosen the right woman for the job.

She did not shrink from her responsibility by using the guise of womanhood or marriage to get out of war. She squarely faced every challenge and overcame manmade obstacles set before her. Fearless leaders will have their character remain intact long after the crisis of war. This special breed of leaders will always take the road less traveled. When others say it cannot be done, they move forward with the purpose of fulfilling their mandate. Every bold leader is always ahead of their time, and that is the reason why they will always be controversial and many times unappreciated by their generation. Deborah was undoubtedly a bold female leader, a woman who sought a way to deliver her people. She refused to live in the past, setting her eyes on the future of a new Israel. Like David, there was a cause, and she was willing to fight for what she believed in.

Great leaders will move forward, even if the rest of the world is resistant to do so. Their boldness is a threat to the conservatives and a breath of freshness to the progressives. Deborah may have moved like a man to many, but she was a woman who found herself in the role of reshaping the world around her, including Israel and the meaning of womanhood altogether.

She recognized people and appreciated them for their individuality and their unique giftings. She provoked others into locating their talents so that they too could make a difference. To save her people, she had to be different, and that required her to be an extremely bold woman. Bold leaders will never live a normal life. They are the ones written about in history books. They are the people that countries honor and holidays are named after. While Deborah never set out to be famous, her boldness ensured that she was. This leader of Israel wanted something better for her people and for her gender. A woman whom many would say had accomplished great things for the Lord. One whose story would be written, a woman as bold as a lion and who won the fight for Israel!

Chapter Eleven

Deborah – A Woman of Integrity

Speak, you who ride on white donkeys, who sit in judges' attire,
and who walk along the road
Judges 5:10-11.

There can be no true leadership without integrity! While your gift brings you before great men, it is your reliability that keeps you in position, and Deborah was just that. Integrity is weighed by one's sincerity as well as fulfilling one's promise, even when faced with opposition and inconvenience. A good leader must always keep her word. Hannah proved to be a great leader by keeping her word to God concerning the dedication of Samuel unto the Lord. For her display of honesty, God gave her five more children. Where there is integrity, there is proof that one is willing to change their reality.

> ෯෬
>
> AN ETHICAL LEADER IS ONE WHO HOLDS HER WORKERS ACCOUNTABLE AND RESPONSIBLE BY THE SAME STANDARDS THAT SHE HOLDS HERSELF.
>
> ෯෬

Integrity means dealing with issues that others have refused to address and making things right with God. A good leader must keep her word at all costs. Deborah proved that she was honorable and reliable in a time when the leaders of Israel walked in dishonesty. She kept her word that she would follow Barak to battle. Her men needed a leader who would be dependable, and she was just that. People of integrity do not renege on promises made. They are known for their transparency, honesty, and nobility of character.

A good leader must display these three characteristics even above their skill or talent. A good leader lives by a certain code of ethics. Deborah was a woman of certain principles and values, and it showed in her decision-making and her relationships with those who were around her. Her values were demonstrated in her daily life; the way she treated her husband, handled the affairs of the state, even her dealings with Barak the general. Her song weaves a story of moral decay in Israel because of a lack of principles until she stood up as a mother in Israel. A principled leader recognizes that she is called to restore spiritual and communal order. A leader who does not take on the same risk as her people is a dictator!

There was nothing inconsistent about Deborah as she proved herself worthy of the title 'leader.' Her heart was inclined to those leaders who were willing to offer themselves up with the people! Esther demonstrated that she was such a leader, and so did Abigail for her husband's servants. Every leader who puts herself at risk for her people will breed loyal followers. Deborah was moved by the plights, struggles, and challenges of her people, and that made her want to serve them all the more. A principled leader wants a better life for all her people. How terribly sad it is to look across certain nations, businesses, and even churches to find out that they do not want a better life for their people.

The crooked president who steals his country's wealth while his people die of hunger while the Madoffs of our generation embezzle people's life savings to live a lie. The pastor who owns ten cars parked in an air-conditioned garage and flies a private jet, while his members walk several miles to attend church. While some in the world see them as leaders, they are men and women who lack integrity. These selfish leaders leave behind the broken lives and dreams of people they were called to serve. Unfortunately, there are more terrible leaders than those who have integrity. An ethical leader is one who holds her workers accountable and at the same standards that she holds herself.

Deborah was a decent leader and she held everyone around her accountable for their actions. When Barak feared to go to war, she informed him that victory would lie in the hands of an unknown woman. A good leader expects her people to lead by example, and sometime when they fail, she must also make them an example as well. Barak's refusal put Deborah in a precarious position; his action would be considered insubordinate as well as defiant by a set of already discouraged army men. A decent leader must also learn not to dwell on the negative but move forward towards the positive.

Deborah dealt with the issue and moved forward. An ethical leader's style of leadership must reflect her own personal and spiritual beliefs, as well as offer a sense of justice and stability to her people. War time is a time of uncertainty, and Deborah's leadership came in a season of great turmoil and insecurity when people needed reassurance and support. Deborah stood for hope and a bright future, and only a leader of integrity can bring about such comfort. Under an ethical leader, job security is established, families flourish, and treaties are signed and kept. One good leader can change the way the entire world receives that nation.

An ethical leader is a mature visionary who understand responsibility. The truth is that not every leader handles responsibility well, and Barak failed in this aspect while Deborah flourished. Barak's response of fear displayed his immaturity, while Jael's ingenuity displayed maturity and grace. A principled leader must understand that sometimes she must walk alone. Deborah had a lonely walk as a leader because of the level of responsibility that God had given to her. Certain tribes of Israel had abandoned them, Barak was threatening to walk away, and all she could do was be totally dependent on God.

Great leaders experience great loneliness even when they are surrounded by a great number of people. A responsible leader is the one God can depend on to get the job done to deliver everyone! A principled leader is a woman who has learned how to think outside of the box.

While Deborah proved to be a great leader, Jael also displayed her ability to break the mold of what and who victory should look like. Ethical leaders understand that the work must be done, whether it is by a man, woman, or child. Flexibility is the first sign of true maturity, and every leader must learn to balance this out. A principled leader is a person of distinction. Deborah stood out because she was an ethical female leader, placed in a unique position in the corrupt nation of Israel. She had the option of doing the same as the other dishonest leaders, but she chose to do things God's way.

Her rarity was noticeable because of the country's delicate situation and her honesty. Her uniqueness brought back honor and prestige to her nation. Every leader must find her individuality that makes her unique, for without it she cannot take her place on the world's stage. Deborah was an honorable leader whose principle was judged through her honest actions. Integrity is God's choice of tool in establishing the new and changing wrong mindsets. Principles introduce change amid opposition and limited resources; the difference one leader can make can be seen by her actions of integrity. And it is for this reason Deborah is hailed as a principled leader of Israel.

Chapter Twelve

Jael – A Resourceful Woman

*Then Jael, Heber's wife took a tent peg and took a hammer in
her hand, and went softly to him and drove the peg into his temple
and it went down into the ground; for he was fast asleep and
weary. So he died.*
Judges 4:21

Any person who takes the initiative without holding a title has the makings of becoming a good leader. While Deborah might have been the leader of Israel, we get to meet Jael, a woman who proved that you do not need a title to display leadership. Sadly, many people in the church refuse to rise as leaders until they are given a title, a position, or have their pastors' approval. While protocol is important, some of the best leaders are wasting away just sitting down in the pews. Women who have buried their talents will have to personally answer to God on Judgment Day for their inaction.

Jael did not need a piece of paper to ordain her or release her into ministry; seeing an opportunity to save her people, she simply seized it and it paid off. Great leaders will always take the lead on unforeseen opportunities. Cleverness is an undeniable asset of a good leader. Jael was a smart woman who proved her smartness and quickness when Sisera appeared, worn and weary, at her doorstep.

A good leader knows when the odds are in her favor and must outwit the

> ಬೋಂಡ
> **A GREAT LEADER CAN NEVER SUCCESSFULLY LEAD BY LOOKING DOWN ON OTHER PEOPLE'S GIFTS, CAREERS, EDUCATION, OR BACKGROUNDS.**
> ಬೋಂಡ

enemy. Sisera never stood a chance, because like Esther after her, Jael never made known her political alliance was to Deborah and not to Sisera. Haman would die at the hands of a woman, and so would Sisera. A leader who can camouflage her true identity and uses wisdom to gain access to her enemy is one who will always win battles! A good leader stays within her area of calling.

Deborah was a judge, prophetess, and military strategist and Jael the housewife, experienced success because they both stayed within the area of their calling. Unfortunately, today's world has successfully and regrettably pitted the housewife against the career woman, stating that a woman must sacrifice one or the other to be successful. The truth is that if both women combine their strength, they can become an unbeatable team. The career woman hails as a great businesswoman, but the world's gives her a *failing grade for picking work over motherhood!* They figure that just because she does not make brownies or wave her children good-bye in the morning that she is both a terrible mother and selfish wife!

The fact of the matter is that every woman is called to achieve different things for God – in ministry , at home and in the marketplace. The Lord saw fit to use Deborah, a judge, prophetess, and a strategist to debunk outdated theories, as we learn that a woman can indeed have everything through careful planning. The world has also been equally intolerant of the self-sacrificing housewife as well! This hardworking woman has been labelled many times as *'unintelligent and too lazy to handle a job.'* This includes the very woman who gave up a six-figure job to be a stay-at-home mother! Seriously people!!! And heaven forbid if there is an instance of divorce and the ex-wife requests alimony and child support! Watch how fast the claws of religious condemnation by both men and women come out to attack her.

The world and even the Church will try and sell the false narrative that the love of a husband and child should be enough payment for that stay-at-home mother. They will tell the housewife that she is worthless and should take any scraps that are handed out to her. They conveniently forget that the housewife is many things – *driver, banker, accountant, doctor, administrator, cleaner, cook, nanny, researcher, athlete, counselor, cheerleader, mother, and lover, all rolled up into one.*

The housewife is no different from the career woman, who must give her best on her job. While the career woman might wear one hat on the job, the housewife must wear multiple hats while juggling every responsibility with some form of expertise without any formalized training! Both types of women are relevant to the kingdom, as God requires the services of both the housewife and the career woman to fulfill His heavenly mandate. Jael is just as important as Deborah the leader! Great leaders will always inspire the Jael's of their generation. Deborah the career woman and Jael the homemaker, though from two vastly different worlds, God uses them both to secure Israel's victory!

It is time for women around the world to put down their guns and join hands together, whether in the marketplace or at the home; each of them have a shared responsibility to one another. The career woman and housewife must become teammates seeking out what is best for each other while helping one another. Sisterhood will never be accomplished if women world-wide do not change their mindset from competition to cooperation. We are not each other's enemy, but rather we are sisters. If we can fundamentally come together and support one another then great things can be attained through the power of unity.

A leader can never successfully lead by looking down on other people's gifts, careers, education, or backgrounds. Jael used the resources that were available to her. What makes one leader better than another is her ability to make the best use of whatever she has around her. Jael proves that she is just as resourceful as her leader, Deborah. Though they had different tools available, each woman was able to aid the other in getting the mission done. Where Deborah's gift jumpstarted the war, it was

Jael's gift that helped to end it! A great leader must know where her gift ends and her counterpart's gift begins! Deborah dealt in the spiritual while Jael used her gift in a practical manner. While Deborah devised a strategy, Jael resorted to the use of ingenuity. Deborah was methodical, while Jael was a quick thinker. Deborah's army used weapons while Jael used household tools!

Had Jael chosen to use a hammer and a tent peg out on the battlefield, it would have been disastrous for Israel and vice-versa for Deborah. A good leader knows that different backgrounds bring with them different gifts of expertise, tools, and wisdom. And this is proven through the Deborah-Jael alliance. These women effectively pooled their individual resources and tools together and turned around the fate of Israel. Now that is what one calls being resourceful!

A good leader has things in common with her followers or helpers. Deborah and Jael were married to men who were not threatened by their individuality. Deborah's husband was supportive about her work, while Jael did not share in her husband's political views but rather sided with Israel. Both women wanted the best for their country and were willing to make personal sacrifices to do so. They also refused to allow gender bias to prevent them from contributing to the uplifting of their country.

Both women fulfilled their obligations without making any excuses. A great leader teaches her people how to use their resources effectively and efficiently to maximize their success in doing the will of God! When the layers are pulled back, the fact is that the career woman and homemaker of today have more in common than they care to realize or investigate! Quite ingeniously, Jael uses her home as the final battleground against Sisera, Israel's archenemy. Women did not fight in those days, and even if they did, Jael would not have been a likely candidate, considering her husband's allegiance to Sisera and his king.

She allowed God to bring the battle to her home. Unskilled in handling a sword but skillful with a hammer, this woman understood the power of a perfect strike in the skull. Sisera stumbling into her tent was to her own advantage and that of her people. Had she been enlisted in the army; Israel would have missed out on its opportunity to kill Sisera. Every denial is not bad news! God instead used the so-called disadvantage of her gender as an occasion to destroy Sisera!

Resourceful leaders know how to turn a terrible situation into a grand opportunity of favor. Resourceful leaders know how to properly assess their enemy's vulnerabilities. Jael carefully measured Sisera's vulnerability as he was weaponless and unprotected making him an easy target!

Everything played into her hands on that day. Her husband was conspicuously absent from the home as Sisera had fled on foot, a rarity for a man of his status and wealth. Jael recognized that she had only one chance of killing Sisera and destabilizing Jabin, the Canaanite king. A good leader sees her enemy's weakness and capitalizes on it! The rather weak, tired, and discouraged Sisera was at Jael's mercy and she was going to do something about it.

Sisera was no longer in control; this same principle applies in corporate take-overs and military invasions. A perception of weakness created the opportunity that Jael so desperately needed to destroy Sisera. The army general's greatest threat was not Barak, but a housewife! A good leader uses all the information that has been handed over to her to make tactical decisions. Like great companies and countries that practice hostile take-overs, Jael used the information that she had gathered about Sisera against him. A resourceful person is normally an informed person, and to become successful one needs correct and relevant information. This is because decisions must be made on facts and not hearsay, as it could be a matter of life or death.

Jael also knew the general well, due to his many visits, his likes, and dislikes. She also gathered indirect intelligence by reading his body language and the fear in his eyes. It was the break that Israel had been hoping for, and she converted all the information presented and made it work for her! A good leader turns reliable information into an opportunity to execute a workable plan. Every good leader knows that she has a race against time. Jael knew that she had little time to execute her plan against Sisera. Time was one thing she did not have. Jabin, enraged about losing the battle, would be in search of his most prized general, Sisera. And Sisera, having lost the battle, would regroup, and return with great vengeance.

With her husband absent, she needed to move quickly. She had to use the most unassuming asset that she had as a woman, and that was her hospitality. She offered him milk in her finest china and a warm blanket, all the while planning the exact time to take him out! A great leader invests in the subject that she is called to annihilate. A good leader chooses her ammunition according to the size of her enemy! Jael had three things in her favor: home advantage, Sisera's trust, and an inconspicuous weapon. A sword or a spear would have alerted her enemy, so she took what was a common household tool and used it. A resourceful leader is a woman who never loses focus on her mission. She systematically set the stage for the assassination of Sisera. A good leader does not always require many women around her to get a particular job work done.

With little time afforded her, Jael single-handedly destroyed the general. Jael did in one day what Israel as a nation could not achieve in twenty years. The right time and resources, along with the right leader, can produce astronomical results. Being a woman played a pivotal role in helping Jael kill Sisera. A good leader must know when her gender can work for her! The general underestimated the power of a woman, especially that of a housewife. History has demonstrated the dangers of underestimating the power of a woman. Abigail saved her household while Esther saved her nation. And it was by the hands of a woman and a millstone that King Abimelech was murdered.

A good leader does not complain about her gender, but rather learns to capitalize on it! Jael used her womanly appeal of hospitality to cater to Sisera's weary needs. The leader who can see her gender as an asset and not a liability will always find a way to succeed. A good leader will stage her attack while her enemy is asleep, and Jael was no different. She chose to use the element of surprise on the unsuspecting but tired war hero called Sisera. Her equipment could not be used while he was awake, as it would prove to be unproductive. But asleep, the hammer and peg would become a lethal weapon.

A resourceful leader uses the tools she has available to win wars. Such a woman will always find a way to complete her assignment. What makes a leader good is her ability to be resourceful; using what is available to create her miracle. She understands that the power of change is in her hands, and she will in turn mold her own destiny; the type of woman who can turn a critical situation around and work it completely to her advantage.

She does not need a title, a position, or recognition to get the job done, but views her gender as an opportunity for a greater platform. She relishes the idea of being underestimated by many because she is secure in who God has made her to be. This woman is not found among the crowd but is her own individual, one who will take her place among future undiscovered legends. As the saying goes, she who laughs last will laugh the best, and Jael becomes the woman who has a whole lot to laugh about!

Chapter Thirteen

Jael – A Woman of Great Hospitality

Most blessed among women is Jael, the wife of Heber the Kenite. Blessed is she among women in tents. He asked for water, she gave milk. She brought out cream in a lordly bowl
Judges 5:24-25

> ෨ා◌ය
>
> WHEN A GOOD LEADER IS UNDERESTIMATED, SHE USES THE POWER OF HOSPITALITY TO HER FAVOR.
>
> ෨ා◌ය

Fine hospitality is what God has given to every woman to be able to win some of her hardest critics. I love the story of Queen Cleopatra, who wagers a bet against the dashing Marc Anthony, inviting him to the most expensive dinner in history. Marc accepts, and at dinner with a single goblet of wine and an empty plate, Cleopatra crushes her large pearl earring, dissolves it in wine, and drinks it. The Roman general is stunned as the cost of one pearl in those days was equivalent to the price of fifteen countries. Marc gracefully conceded to Cleopatra in an age-old art of hospitality that has lost its appeal to many modern-day women.

Yet countless women throughout history and the Bible have used this art form to gain an advantage for God and saved households. At the feast prepared by Queen Esther for her husband, it was at the dinner table she was able to mention the murderous plot against her people, and Haman is hung. It was the kindness that the Shulammite woman had extended to the prophet of God that gave her an unexpected miracle of a son. The generosity of Abigail wins the heart of David and spares her household from bloodshed.

By the cool drink of Rebecca, the heart of Abraham's old servant is won and secures her marriage to Isaac, his only son. Hospitality has been one of the main ways that God has given as a tool for women, and yet many have distained it, missing out on the blessings that come attached with it. A great leader uses hospitality as a door opener and an icebreaker! Throughout the Bible, there are records of unprecedented miracles that came about due to the use of hospitality. When the widow of Zarephath baked a cake of bread for Elijah the runaway prophet, she and her household were spared in the time of famine.

Abigail brought food to David and his men, and eleven days later, she became his wife! Deborah's song introduces the world to Jael's homely side; a woman who disarms her enemy not by a sword, but through the weaponry of hospitality. She extended her friendship to Sisera by using her culinary gifts. A great leader must determine how she handles a threat; it could be with a sword or using kind words. Jael used the right words to lure Sisera to his death. When he needed a place to hide, she covered him with a blanket; when he asked for water, she gave him warm milk instead. When he asked for her to be his eyes, she assured him protection.

A good leader extends herself, knowing that she has one chance for victory! With every help offered, Sisera continued to lower his guard and trust Jael; her warm reception placed him at ease and threw him off guard. Hospitality means going beyond what is expected of you for someone who needs help. A great leader gives her best, knowing that it will always give her an additional edge over her enemies! What did Jael use to guarantee the death of Israel's enemy? She used the best of what she had in her house. She used honey-coated words to draw in her enemy, while an unwise woman would have resorted to harsh words. She served her enemy the best, while an unwise woman would have given Sisera her leftovers.

She used the subtle approach of giving her best and it is what killed her enemy. How unfortunate that we offer our leftovers and expect the best from God. Even the wicked general appreciated what Jael offered because he recognized it was her best, and she was able to win him over! The leader who gives her best will never go un-rewarded! Jael's legacy was birthed by her outstanding hospitality, and God rewarded her for it. Hospitality has to do with *consideration, reaction, and provision.* It shows a level of concern about an issue; one's reaction to that issue and the ability to address that need through proper provision. A good leader addresses all three components in dealing with hospitality.

Dorcas is a prime example, a woman who never preached a sermon but is recorded for her good works and charitable contributions to an entire city. When she died, there was tangible proof of her hospitality that brought her back to life. While Jael might not have had a voice, her hospitality became her open door. A good leader lets her hospitality speak up for her. When a good leader is underestimated, she uses the power of hospitality to her favor.

There are several women in the Bible who have been despised, underestimated, or undervalued, but who used hospitality to secure their personal victory. Rahab the prostitute warmly received and hid the spies of Israel. She was in a dishonorable profession, but there was a leader hidden inside of her. A good leader is not always included in the political decision-making of her time. The truth is that not every great leader has been invited to sit at the table of power. While many people are recognized for their leadership abilities, there are hundreds more who may never be recognized formally as leaders.

Jael was a leader in the making. Although she was a housewife, it became inconceivable that such a woman would be responsible for the death of Sisera, one of the greatest generals of his time. A good leader comes in all types of different packages. Until the church learns from biblical history and world events that some of the most influential and greatest men have owed their downfall to the power of hospitality, the church will continue in empty victories. Hospitality can be used in the arena of God to advance His cause, and yet at the same time destroy our age-old nemesis, Satan.

If the Christian woman abandons her gift of warm reception, she will continue to experience insignificant success in the kingdom. Jael, the overlooked housewife, employed the art of hospitality to gain the confidence of a wicked army general, and killed him. This could only happen because men like Sisera underestimated the assets of an exceptionally good female leader.

Chapter Fourteen

Jael – The Handy Housewife

She stretched her hand to the tent peg, her right hand to the workmen's hammer. She pounded Sisera, she pierced his head, she split and struck through his temple. At her feet he sank, he fell, he lay still. At her feet, he fell, where he sank, there he fell dead.
Judges 5:26-27

An incredibly good leader must also be a handy one! Jael was not only a resourceful and , quick-witted woman, but she was also very practical. Her quick-thinking nature turned an ordinary household tool into a deadly weapon. Very few people of faith have proven themselves to be versatile and adaptable. Flexibility to your every changing circumstance will lead you into achieving tremendous successes and wins where others failed.

> ෨෬
>
> MANY UNCONVENTIONAL BIBLICAL VICTORIES WERE SECURED BY UNCONVENTIONAL METHODS; THE WOMAN KILLED ABIMELECH WITH A MILLSTONE, SALOME GOT JOHN THE BAPTIST BEHEADED WITH A DANCE, AND ESTHER GOT HAMAN HUNG AFTER EATING AT HER BANQUET.
>
> ෨෬

A good leader uses whatever she has within reach to map out her destiny as adaptability is a sign of faith in God. A good leader uses her originality to produce a great legacy. When creativity entered the home of the indebted prophet's wife through a jar of oil, God gave her a financial empire and her future became secured. Rebecca's pitcher created her opportunity and introduced her to Abraham's servant and her future husband, Isaac.

By the initiative of the Shulammite woman wanting to build a room for the prophet of God, she is honored at her old age with a son. All these women used instruments that they had been given to create a dynasty. The most unconventional tool is what God uses to bless a good leader. A good leader is a woman who knows how to use hospitality, creativity, and flexibility to gain authority. Resourceful people use the resources around them to get great things done. While the expert needs a budget to get the work done, the resourceful uses an insignificant instrument and wars are won. The resourceful tends to be inexperienced but uses creativity to gain the upper hand out of necessity.

Creative minds tend to be self-sufficient because of a lack of support, faith, or finance. While these reasons prevent the experts from doing their jobs, they never stop the resourceful from moving forward. A good leader should also be a great innovator. Where there is an invention, there lies a leader with a great imagination! While there are specialized fields like medicine, engineering, remote sensing etc...that require formal education, there are a lot of other areas where being resourceful can give you the upper hand. Mastery has nothing to do with necessity. Jael could not handle a sword, nor did she have the military strategy of Deborah, but she knew how to handle a hammer and peg skillfully.

In desperation, God makes us produce innovations, and Jael was no different. This does not negate the importance of skillful people or the use of technology, but when all else fails and time is of the essence then human ingenuity is necessary. A resourceful leader effectively uses the tools that are around her. Jael did not wish that she could handle a sword at that time, the tool she needed was in her workbench; what is easily accessible and in plain sight will be used to achieve the ultimate victory.

Many unconventional biblical victories were secured by unconventional methods; the woman killed Abimelech with a millstone, Salome got John the Baptist beheaded with a dance, and Esther got Haman hung after eating at her banquet. Conventional weaponry does not necessarily guarantee you the victory but using what God has given you in your hands does. A good leader knows that God creates the opportunity for her to use her God-given weaponry. A resourceful leader understands the power of time and opportunity. Jael had a small window of opportunity to kill Sisera, there was no time to leave the tent and seek help. She had to seize the moment; because once he woke up, he would recover and defeat Israel.

With a race against time, there was only one chance to gain the victory for her people, and so she acted accordingly. Resourceful leaders use instruments that are functional and available! Jael utilized a user-friendly household instrument that was also in mint condition; the hammer and peg proved to be multifunctional! The standard use of these instruments that held down the tent will now hold down a mighty general! A resourceful leader understands the power of the multifaceted. The prophet's bed turned multifunctional when the Shulammite woman laid her dead son on it, and he recovered. The Red Sea functioned as a walkway for Israel and a watery grave for the Egyptians. A good leader who discovers the dual functionality of her gift will receive compensation for using it! Jael's gift not only saved Israel, but it also lifted her as a heroine.

Jael was in complete control of her gift; she handled the hammer and the peg. They were not awkward or heavy, but they responded well to her touch. A good leader is never given a gift that she is unable to handle. Jael had mastered her gift and had control over it because she was in constant use of it. A resourceful leader will always appreciate her tools and must be willing to use them. Jael valued her instruments, and because she used them differently, she stood out distinguished from among her peers. No leader will be recognized without the use of their tools or talent.

The leader whose gift remains unrecognized and unused is a woman of great tragedy and has allowed for wasted opportunities. When Jael chose to use her gift, she went down in history as the woman who killed a general. A good leader knows that every gift cannot work independently of another. Jael's gift could not be fully utilized until she had put Sisera to sleep with the use of warm milk and a blanket; her household tools were useless if he were awake. A good leader uses every tool that has been made available to her. Jael used every opportunity and tools wisely and methodically the day that Sisera entered her home. With his reflexes and his reaction time down, she struck him dead.

When the prophecy said that he would be sold into the hands of a woman, it never mentioned what type of woman or her occupation. A good leader will always fulfill a prophetic word of God. One thing for sure and that is for generations to come, Sisera the great general would be remembered as a man who died under a warm blanket and by the hands of a housewife who used a peg and sledgehammer!

Chapter Fifteen

Deborah, Barak and Jael – Teamwork

Then the mother of Sisera looked through the window, and cried out through the lattice, Why is his chariot so long in coming? Why tarries the clatter of his chariots?
Judges 5:28

A good leader understands the power of teamwork. Deborah would have never achieved the success she did without Barak and Jael. Teamwork requires everyone putting together their skills for a common goal. Barak may not have been a prophet nor was Jael a judge, but both stepped up to the plate when it was required of them. Cohesiveness is a very necessary ingredient for a successful team, whether it is marriage, ministry, or working within a company.

The best and first team that ever existed was and remains the Trinity, and what a great team! A good team leader can accomplish

> ଓଅ
>
> DEBORAH HAD A GREAT TEAM WHOSE ACTIONS WERE SYNCHRONIZED BY THE HOLY SPIRIT. WHILE SHE AND BARAK WERE OUT IN THE BATTLEFIELD, JAEL WAS STRATEGICALLY IN HER TENT WAITING FOR SISERA TO WALK IN
>
> ଓଓ

great things wherever her team location might be! Deborah had a great team whose actions were synchronized by the Holy Spirit. While she and Barak were out in the battlefield, Jael was strategically in her tent as though waiting for Sisera to walk in. While they were on Mount Tabor, Jael was in Zaanaim. Every great team has a shared vision and can work out of different locations.

A great leader who understands her job description is not defined by a difference of location. The strength of every team is tested by how much they can achieve working from a distance. A team leader who has made her vision clear becomes an inspiration to people everywhere. Deborah, Barak, and Jael all wanted the same thing for their country, which was freedom. While she shared military strategies with Barak, Deborah shared the bond of womanhood with Jael. A good leader knows how to form powerful coalitions by building the right relationships. There was a commonality between all three of them; Deborah was meant to turn Israel back to God, Barak to win a war, and Jael to kill Sisera the general.

With great teamwork each person can achieve a common goal! A good team leader seeks for great collaboration among her peers. Deborah understood the power of group effort. It required every team member doing what was clearly expected of them. To be part of a group, you must fulfill your responsibilities; Deborah rallied the troops, Barak went to war, and God led Sisera into the tent of Jael to finish the job. A good team does not fight one another but follows orders and uses whatever is necessary to be successful. A good team knows that they are incomplete without each other. Victory was attainable because of Barak's and Jael's cooperation.

A good team leadership can only go as far as her team is in complete agreement! There can be no team without an agreement, and that is what Deborah had with her people. Harmony is needed for any group to win; differences must be handled before the execution of a plan and not during it! Unresolved issues in any team will negatively impact the desired outcome of it. Barak agreed with the war while Jael concurred with Deborah, even though she had never met her. Show me a great team and I will show you a team leader who inspires unity! A good team leader is a woman who knows how to inspire!

Deborah knew how to motivate her team. She encouraged Barak to go to war when others refused. She stirred up hope in a housewife called Jael, whom she did not personally know. Every team needs a reason or motive behind what they are doing, something to believe in, and with the right leader; a little team can suddenly become a worldwide movement! A good team leader builds her team with people who understand commitment. A team of committed people is a team that can accomplish the impossible! Deborah knew this about her team. A team leader who does not use commitment as a determining factor to weed out the uncommitted is heading for failure.

Deborah's team was committed, they did not offer up excuses even though they could have. Barak was asked to fight a war without adequate weaponry, putting him at a disadvantage. Jael could have used the excuse of supporting her husband's political beliefs, but she broke ranks for what she believed to be the calling of God and killed Sisera, her husband's friend. A person might have faith, but that does not translate into commitment. A committed team gets the work done without any excuses. A good team leader makes sure that everyone understands their role. A good team has people who fulfill different responsibilities; every role is important in achieving maximum victory. Every role is vital in a team; without students, a teacher is unable to teach, and without a teacher the students cannot learn.

While leadership is a significant role in and of itself, it has no value if there are no people to lead. Deborah, Barak, and Jael made a great team because everyone fulfilled their duties, and they were all rewarded. When a team leader has the right character, team spirit will flourish, and God will always get the glory. Every team carries the spirit of its leader, whether she is good or bad, and Deborah had a great spirit. She did not mind sharing the stage with Barak and Jael, the unknown housewife. If she did, then God would have never used her to prophesy that the war would be won by a woman. Insecurities, selfishness, and high-mindedness must be done away to work as a team.

A good team is one that has been given the opportunity to form a camaraderie or closeness. Deborah's team was in sync; no one would have believed that Jael had not been recruited to kill Sisera. A good leader builds her team carefully, enabling them to function like a well-oiled machine. A good team leader knows that the team is a unit, to fail or succeed as one, because there is no individuality in a good team. While a leader is ultimately held responsible for the failure or success of her team, there is no "I" but rather "we." The truth is that many times the success or failure of a team may rest squarely on a faceless person or one without rank or prestige.

Jael was that team member, a nonentity who could even be considered a traitor by her husband's alliance to Sisera. Yet, she rightly calculated the deep breathing of Sisera to kill him. The greatest team is one in which an unknown gets the job done successfully! God loves to work through a team, and He chose to use Deborah, Barak, and Jael. By worldly standards, they would be a horrible choice at that time, an untried female leader, a failed general, and a housewife. But God was out to debunk the theory that a woman could not lead, and it would take thousands of years later for women to be recruited into armies and allowed to work for fire departments. And yes, one day even become a world president!

The greatness of any team is dependent on the spirit of the woman who is leading it, and Deborah proves that women and men can work together and build an unstoppable team. If I were to name Deborah, Barak, and Jael, I would dub them the *'DREAM TEAM OF GOD.'* If God has given you a dream as a woman, all that you need is the right team to make it a reality!

Chapter Sixteen

Deborah - A Woman of Commitment and Focus

Speak you who ride on white donkeys. Who sit in judge's attire, and who walk along the road? Far from the noise of archers, among the watering places, there they shall recount the righteous acts of the Lord. The righteous acts for His villagers in Israel; then the people of the Lord shall go down to the gates.
Judges 5:10-11

A committed leader is a focused leader. Deborah had unbroken focus and unwavering commitment as a leader. It showed in her approach to everything and everyone around her. A good leader honors commitment when everyone else is bailing. A focused leader is a woman who is not in pursuit of a name or fame but ends up becoming famous because of her focus. Deborah achieved them both, because your commitment tells the world what your cause is while your focus tells them what you are willing to pay to attain it. Deborah was ready to die for her cause and make the necessary sacrifices that was required.

> ⟡⟡
> A GOOD LEADER KNOWS THAT SHE CAN NEVER WIN A BATTLE WITH THE UNCOMMITTED BUT DEPENDS ON THOSE WHO ARE ROOTING FOR HER.
> ⟡⟡

A focused leader must prove that she is single-minded and self-motivated. Deborah is proof, like most good leaders that people must learn to inspire themselves when others have quit on them. Israel had lost its focus and therefore lost her commitment to God. Part of Deborah's assignment was to keep her focus to get the Israelites back to renewing their commitment to the Lord. This could only be realized by killing Sisera in battle. She had no one to support her except for her husband and God, but she kept her focus.

A committed leader is focused on getting the task done. Very few leaders will ever have followers who will inspire them; they must increase their level of enthusiasm themselves and not rely on others to do it for them. A focused leader tackles any issues that prevents the work from getting done and does not avoid them. Regrettably, the world teaches us to avoid issues of confrontation when there is a desperate task at hand. The leader who refuses to deal with leadership issues at once will be forced to deal with them at an inappropriate or most critical moment. Deborah dealt with issues and resolved them aptly.

A focused leader knows what methods best suit her people. Deborah used encouragement to get Barak to go to war, while Jael needed inspiration to kill Sisera. A good leader is a woman who is hands-on. A committed leader has an eye for detail, a good leader must learn how to delegate and understand that one missing detail can determine the success or failure of a mission, and Deborah was thorough in this area. She did not leave anything to chance, as she specifically told Barak what God expected from him and his men on Mount Tabor. A committed leader does not allow anyone to straddle the fence.

There is no room for spectatorship, but participation is a known requirement for dealing with serious leaders. Such leaders have no tolerance for confusion or inconsistencies. When Deborah realized that some of the other tribes wanted to speculate and not participate in the war, she left them alone and worked with what she had. A good leader knows that she can never win a battle with the uncommitted but depends on those who are rooting for her. A focused leader is the driving force behind every movement. Deborah was the nucleus; the person who could take Israel to its next level. It was her focus that made her go to war with her men, and it was the same commitment that ensured she made the right types of decisions.

A focused leader is a woman bent on restoring pride and honor where it has been lost. Deborah would exemplify the new type of Israel, one of integrity, tenacity, and commitment to God. Every committed leader has their life shaped by some type of encounter, divine or otherwise. While there is no record of Deborah having a 'Damascus moment,' I do believe that every good leader has one. It is the reason behind their drive and commitment. It is this moment that changes them forever, transforming them into agents of change. Their entire perspective changes, and so does the direction of their life as well.

When committed people discover a cause, they map their destiny in its direction, not afraid of pursuing, it no matter the cost! Deborah's encounter with God not only fueled her passion but prepared her for leadership. A committed leader has a knack for gathering the right people together for the job! Good leaders must be compassionate but also ruthless as they build their team methodically. They sever unproductive relationships and fiercely protect and nurture the right ones. Deborah understood this concept and used it, because she knew that you are only as good as the team that you have put together.

Every good team should have some experts, and yet there needs to be room for innovators and plenty of opportunity for those who have proven to be faithful. A committed leader rather nurtures the teachable, reachable, and faithful, then deals with the difficult, impossible, or able. Every good leader should remember that God would rather use the faithful than use the able! A dedicated leader wants to know one thing, and that is if you can get the job done. Focused leaders are not interested in how many degrees you have or who you worked for, but rather the quality of your work and if you can get things done.

Deborah was no different, as I believe that she chose Barak, though he was fearful, because he was also able and flexible. A good leader wants the work done with as few casualties as possible! Bad leaders are distracted by name-dropping and fancy titles, while focused leaders are constantly weighing all other possible options. With a focused leader, you have one opportunity to make a good impression, or she will choose another person to get the job done. A committed leader will break protocol when the lives of many are in danger. Deborah was a woman who understood protocol, but like many other women, there were times she was forced to break, as in prophesying that the war would be ended by a woman.

When lives hang in the balance, a loyal leader must choose between tradition and compassion, the accusation of men or the word of God. Queen Esther chose to break protocol and approach the king. Abigail risked the wrath of her husband and the accusations of her city by sneaking out to meet David without an escort as a married woman. Mary the mother of Jesus was willing to risk the shame of being a single mother to give birth to the Savior. A focused leader looks at the whole picture, while little people whisper and point fingers! Every blade of grass, every sparkling star that presses against the velvet of night and the baby elephant that nestles close to her mother show the focus and the commitment of God.

He took His time with creation, taking every detail into account, showing not only His involvement but also His unfailing love for mankind. God was genuinely interested in the plight of Israel and made sure that Deborah would secure their victory. He had given her all the necessary tools to turn things around. His only requirement was her focus and commitment. With these two attributes, she would be unstoppable, and this was His commitment to her.

Chapter Seventeen

Deborah, Barak, and Jael – Recognized

Awake, awake Deborah! Awake, awake, sing a song!
Arise, Barak, and lead your captives away
O son of Abinoam
Judges 5:12

> **ℰℛ**
>
> GREAT LEADERS ARE DISSATISFIED UNTIL THEY EXTEND THEIR SPHERE OF INFLUENCE TO HELPING OTHERS.
>
> **ℰℛ**

In the top three leading movie industries today; Hollywood (US), Bollywood (India) and Nollywood (Nigeria), Deborah, Barak and Jael would be considered breakout stars, people who would be bankable, and they would be right! They are what movies are made of as a team: a female judge, an unsure general, and a regular housewife brought change to Israel and became famous for it. What this simply means is that they are recognized for the contributions that they made in their nation. These three people who were underestimated by many rose to the top by working as a team!

As partners they attained great success, while perhaps working alone they would have failed in killing Sisera. A good leader must wake up to the fact that God has called her! Deborah, Barak, and Jael are all leaders because they woke up to the fact that their country needed their service. Deborah was already stirred up, but she had to rouse up Barak to his own position. And Jael had to wake up to the fact that a woman could also make a difference! A good leader wakes up the uninspired leaders around her. All three of them become recognized because they not only woke up but made an impact in their nation.

Their accomplishment introduced them. Uninspired leaders will remain unrecognized generals. A good leader changes the standard of what people define as a good working relationship. Deborah demonstrated that women leaders could work successfully with a man without his masculinity being threatened or disrespected. She also discredited the myth that women cannot work well together. Individually, these three people would have remained unrecognizable, but as a team they were an unbeatable force to contend with and they were invaluable. Deborah shows that as their leader, more could be achieved corporately than individually, and that some of the best alliances are the types that are unappreciated and underrated.

A good team is an unforgettable team! Three of them would be remembered and hailed for their great exploits, despite their era, gender, limited weaponry, tribe abandonment, and the great hardship they each faced. They rose above their nation's dilemma and became great. A recognizable team is one that gives each person a chance to become something. God uses our individual challenges to give inspiration to a future generation. Although they were from different backgrounds, each of them allowed the other room enough to make an impact that would be worthwhile.

Deborah had to show that she was a good enough leader; Barak had to display that he could be a general, and Jael had to show that a woman could get the job done. And together their achievements were recorded. A good leader and her people will eventually become national heroes. All three of them became household names because of their heroic actions, even though it was never their plan to become well-known. They must have suffered as the butt of many jokes, from first female leader to weaponless general to the housewife whose husband supported Israel's enemy. Despite all their challenges, they still ended up victorious as well as famous.

A recognizable leader uses her fame to make great changes. Every one of them now had the opportunity to positively impact other people's lives. Being famous allows you to lend your voice to good causes. Impact players do not stop working because they have hit a certain measure of success, but they continue to change their community, nation, and even the world to become a better place. Great leaders are dissatisfied until they extend their sphere of influence to helping others. Barak became the symbol of hope for small armies that did not have enough weapons, while Deborah and Jael challenged women to get up and make an impact. Such people are able to change the mindset of people around them and bring about an awareness and movement.

Victory brings about the realization of unfair practices and how they affect a group or set of people. One can be certain that after the death of Sisera, some people began to appreciate female leadership, while others recognized that it takes a special gift to work with a skeleton army, and others started to respect the power of the housewife. Identifiable leaders can demystify certain ideas about who is qualified to be a leader, thus disproving conservative and biased critics. In one day, these three leaders removed stigmas, warped philosophies, and backward ideologies, and opened the door to endless possibilities for other men and women in their nation to have a chance at success.

When we work together, what was once impossible becomes attainable, and God used Deborah to prove that. A good leader is one who uses the power of accomplishment to build communal relationships. When hidden talents and strengths are revealed, the ordinary person becomes a heroine. Success brings to light understanding, dialogue, tolerance, and most of all, compassion. Recognition makes people embrace their differences and not fight against them. Your gender, race, language, country and yes even religion might be different, but your challenges, struggles, pain, and joy are very much the same. The power of success makes us realize that we have more in common than we realize.

Deborah, Barak, and Jael may have been vastly different in gift, style, and gender but they were remarkably similar in goals and ambitions. Impact players have no time to waste, nor do they make room for discrimination! A great leader learns when to shift the responsibility for taking care of their country to its people. While Deborah, Barak, and Jael may have been chosen by God to kill Sisera, the people had to learn to share in the responsibility in ensuring their liberty. The victory taught the people that Israel was their nation and that they could not depend on others for their freedom, but only themselves.

An influential leader tactfully develops ways of helping to ensure that other people take up the reins of national responsibility and motivates them to become committed. A great leader strengthens the resolve of her people by teaching them to believe in each other which ultimately produces a powerful nation. Every good leader must have a spirit of forgiveness. Winning has a way of producing new alliances, and some of your worst critics will turn around one day to become some of your greatest allies. Though it is never mentioned, I am sure that Deborah won certain people over by having won the war against Sisera.

Every good leader will always prayerfully look out for the fruits of repentance and make sure such people prove themselves. Where there is fame, there also comes with it acceptance and criticism, as well as admiration. These three leaders became recognizable, not just because they won the war, but by what method God used them to do so.

Each of them also had their own personal challenges that individually they all had to overcome to work together as a collective. While their individual limitations were well-documented, they never once doubted themselves or even consider their shortcomings as a hindrance or use them as an excuse for failure. In the end, I am sure that many people of Israel respected them more for overcoming personal shortcomings and what they had suffered had greater significance than for they had accomplished. While many will seek the accolades of men, Deborah, Barak, and Jael prove that when God recognizes you, it comes with uncontestable benefits!

Chapter Eighteen

Deborah – The Peacemaker

So, the land had rest for forty years
Judges 5:31

A good leader knows the value of peace and will do anything to achieve it. While it might seem like a contradiction that Deborah was a peacemaker, being that she was called to lead Israel to war, the truth was that Israel could not experience peace until Sisera was dead. God had chosen her to establish peace, and sometime fighting is necessary to put an end to turmoil, confusion, slavery, and disorder for the promotion of peace. Peace was crucial for Israel after twenty years of chaos and slavery. God required a peace broker in the form of an unlikely candidate, a woman called Deborah.

A good leader uses the power of persuasion to win over the right people. Deborah was gifted in this area as she used her ability to win over Barak the general. It was the same gift she must have used in judging all her cases. Every leader is currently using her primary gift in one way or the other. A peaceful leader champions peaceful negotiation and walks in the office of reconciliation and restoration.

> ଶୋ୯ଃ
>
> A GOOD LEADER KNOWS THAT FIGHTING FOR PEACE WILL BRING ABOUT NEW AND STRATEGIC RELATIONSHIPS, NATIONAL INFRASTRUCTURE, AND POLITICAL STABILITY WITHIN HER BORDERS.
>
> ଶୋ୯ଃ

As backslidden as Israel was, Deborah had to change her tactics to win these rebellious people back to God. It would take the skill of peace and reconciliation. Her gift had no boundaries, as it must have made an impact on a housewife called Jael who also wanted peace for Israel. A peaceful leader is always looking to the future. Deborah the peacemaker had a responsibility to ensure that the present-day calamity of Israel did not repeat itself in the future. Good leaders broker peace on every level. A good leader sends out peacekeepers or delegations to finalize peace treaties with their enemies. While there was no way to achieve peace with Sisera, Jael indirectly became the peace representative of her nation by inviting him to seek refuge within her tent.

Peace brokers are skillful at working both sides of the table, seeking resolution without compromising the integrity of God's message. It was through peace that Jael was able to destroy Sisera, who had no clue that she was out to kill him. A good leader must become a great mediator and is a public servant. Deborah was God's emissary. Recognizing that there was no hope of tranquility between Israel and Canaan, she would need the help of others to establish peace. A diplomatic leader must cultivate strategic alliances that will broker or lead ultimately to peace. Without it, misunderstanding and uncertainty will plague a nation, but where there is rest, there is great confidence.

A savvy leader knows that if she establishes peace, there will be national stability. Deborah had a lot on her plate as a peacemaker, and she knew it. For any country to be productive, it must have stability, which can only be arrived at through peace. Peace means that the country can build solid infrastructure, create jobs, and market stabilization, and a country that was once considered nothing can turn into a superpower. The income of people rises, and the quality of life improves for the whole nation.

If Israel were to be respected and taken seriously by her enemies, she would need stability. It is by this that governments can control their countries and order is seen by all. A tactful leader knows that peace eradicates poverty and fear out of a society. Deborah had to win two wars, one against Sisera and the other against poverty. Her leadership was about to be tested in prosperity, for without it, no leader could ever remain in office. A good leader knows that fighting for peace will bring about new and strategic relationships.

The truth is that battle-ridden countries do not make for lasting friendships, due to unstable governments, and it became imperative that Deborah be given a chance to forge new alliances and rebuild damaged ones. This could be seen in the choice of Heber aligning with Sisera instead of Israel. Jael's decision helped end their division. A good leader knows that peace produces balance in her nation.

The presence of violence is the absence of peace, and so injustice, division, and idolatry thrive in such an environment. Unity allows everyone to have a voice in their communities.

Peaceful leaders know that everyone deserves the same chance as her sister, and success is achievable. Deborah was a symbol of fairness of opportunity for all women, single or married, rich or poor, educated, or unschooled; she helped bring about equilibrium and allowed her people to make their own choices. A good leader not only brings about liberty but also embraces diversity. Deborah was a peaceful leader who taught her people how to be open to alternatives. Once there is unity, people are permitted to speak out about their different preferences that were at one time not available.

A peaceful leader becomes the catalyst for new discoveries. Deborah planted the seed of innovation within her people; Barak fought using the elements of the weather; while Jael creatively used a hammer to kill the general. Peace is the key to modernization and advancement of any nation, but it is the responsibility of its leader to ensure it. A peaceful leader will always empower her people. Deborah saw a different future for Israel, an empowered nation that would thrive by establishing peace within its borders. A good leader can make sound decisions when they are not always at war.

While every leader knows that part of her call is putting out fires, good solutions are possible when there is peace and tranquility to make sound judgment. Where there is stillness, clear and precise decisions can be made without the doubts of confusion or fatal consequences. Harmony is an attribute that every leader must be willing to die for to obtain it! A great leader knows that without peace, any sign of victory is temporary. Deborah understood that concept and realized that they would have to continue to fight until their people experienced permanent rest; there can be no rest without peace, and she knew this. Finally, peace is one of the sure promises of God that He gave to His disciples.

Great leadership is justly weighed on the scales of peace and how much they pursued it while they were in office. Deborah's legacy ends in the establishment of peace; the measurement of great leadership by both God and man's standards. She may have never realized her impact as a female leader and judge. Her story should inspire women everywhere as she proves herself the ultimate woman leader; one in pursuit of peace.

Conclusion

What Type of Leader Will You Be?

This story concludes with one vital question that every woman must ask herself, and that is what type of leader will you be? You can complain about life's choices and its great inequality or decide that you will rewrite your own story because you have been equipped to make history.

As this chapter closes and the lights fade out, I leave the rest of this page empty for you to start a brand-new story; yours. I pray that you will not only unlock the Deborah inside of you but discover the leader that is within you. And I too end on this peaceful note.

I will be ....

SALVATION PRAYER

Perhaps you have read this book today and have realized that you are not where you are supposed to be in your relationship with Jesus Christ or you may have even backslidden. Here is an opportunity to say the sinner's prayer to get things right with Him and begin to end the pattern of dysfunction in your life.

Heavenly Father, today I invite you into my life to commit my will, my spirit and my soul over to you. I acknowledge that I am a sinner and I am sorry for the sins that I have committed in the past and request your forgiveness.

I confess Jesus Christ as my personal Lord and Savior. I believe in your only begotten son Jesus Christ and that by the shedding of His blood at the Cross of Calvary, my sins have been washed away and I stand as a new creature in Christ Jesus because I have fully believed. I believe in the baptism, death and resurrection of Jesus Christ and that my life is hidden in Christ and I am now saved.

I now thank Jesus for His undying love and grace at the Cross and that I have access to the throne of grace in the time of trouble and tribulation. I also accept the Holy Spirit as the guide and teacher of my life through this new and wonderful journey of abundant life. Lord, transform my life and mold me into what you want me to be now that I am saved. Amen